NOLO *Your Legal Companion*

"In Nolo you can trust." —**THE NEW YORK TIMES**

OUR MISSION
Make the law as simple as possible, saving you time, money and headaches.

Whether you have a simple question or a complex problem, turn to us at:

NOLO.COM

Your all-in-one legal resource

Need quick information about wills, patents, adoptions, starting a business—or anything else that's affected by the law? **Nolo.com** is packed with free articles, legal updates, resources and a complete catalog of our books and software.

NOLO NOW

Make your legal documents online

Creating a legal document has never been easier or more cost-effective! Featuring Nolo's Online Will, as well as online forms for LLC formation, incorporation, divorce, name change—and many more! Check it out at **http://nolonow.nolo.com**.

NOLO'S LAWYER DIRECTORY

Meet your new attorney

If you want advice from a qualified attorney, turn to Nolo's Lawyer Directory—the only directory that lets you see hundreds of in-depth attorney profiles so you can pick the one that's right for you. Find it at **http://lawyers.nolo.com**.

ALWAYS UP TO DATE

Sign up for **NOLO'S LEGAL UPDATER**

Old law is bad law. We'll email you when we publish an updated edition of this book—sign up for this free service at nolo.com/legalupdater.

Find the latest updates at **NOLO.COM**

Recognizing that the law can change even before you use this book, we post legal updates during the life of this edition at **nolo.com/updates**.

Is this edition the newest? **ASK US!**

To make sure that this is the most recent edition available, just give us a call at **800-728-3555**.

(Please note that we cannot offer legal advice.)

Please note

We believe accurate, plain-English legal information should help you solve many of your own legal problems. But this text is not a substitute for personalized advice from a knowledgeable lawyer. If you want the help of a trained professional—and we'll always point out situations in which we think that's a good idea—consult an attorney licensed to practice in your state.

5th edition

Quick & Legal Will Book

by Attorney Denis Clifford

FIFTH EDITION	MAY 2008
Editor	BETSY SIMMONS
Cover Design	SUSAN PUTNEY
Production	MARGARET LIVINGSTON
Proofreader	MARK NIGARA
CD-ROM Preparation	ELLEN BITTER
Index	BAYSIDE INDEXING SERVICE
Printing	CONSOLIDATED PRINTERS, INC.

Clifford, Denis.
Quick & legal will book / by Denis Clifford. -- 5th edition.
p. cm.
ISBN-13: 978-1-4133-0861-7 (pbk.)
ISBN-10: 1-4133-0861-9 (pbk.)
1. Wills--United States--Popular works. 2. Wills--United States--Forms. I. Title.
KF755.Z9C55 2008
346.7305'04--dc22

2007051651

Quantity sales: For information on bulk purchases or corporate premium sales, please contact the Special Sales Department. For academic sales or textbook adoptions, ask for Academic Sales. Call 800-955-4775 or write to Nolo, 950 Parker Street, Berkeley, CA 94710.

Dedication

For my mother, Katherine Corbett Clifford. As her brother said when they were young, "Not like the other girls."

Acknowledgments

Once again, writing and revising a Nolo book was a group effort and could not have been done without the contributions of many of my colleagues here. Specifically, my current editor, Betsy Simmons; previous editors Shae Irving and Steve Elias; Mike Edwards and Ling Yu, of Nolo Press Customer Service, who gave time generously to read and review the original manuscript; Nancy Erb for her wizard-work with computers, doing the layout for the original book. Finally, I want to thank all my fellow Noloids. Each one truly contributes to making this enterprise both productive and such an enjoyable place to work or party.

About the Author

Denis Clifford is a lawyer who specializes in estate planning and practices in Berkeley, California. He is the author of several Nolo books, including *Nolo's Simple Will Book* and *Plan Your Estate*. A graduate of Columbia Law School, where he was an editor of The Law Review, he has practiced law in various ways and is convinced that people can do much of the legal work they need themselves.

Table of Contents

Appendixes

Index

Your Legal Companion for Making a Will

So, you're thinking about writing a will —good for you! Many of us know it's something we should do, but we just never get around to it. After all, we're all busy and have lots of chores just waiting to be tackled.

Happily, if you've decided that now's the right time to finally buckle down, you can make your will easily with the *Quick & Legal Will Book*. This book is for people who want to prepare a basic will in the least amount of time. The basic wills in this book allow you to leave your property simply and clearly, without complicated and unnecessary legal jargon.

You can also use these wills to name guardians for your children and their property. If you're like most parents, you want to make sure that you choose the most caring, competent people to raise your children if something were to happen to you. And you also want to ensure that in that situation, a responsible person will manage your child's finances. Preparing a simple will is the best way to name who you want to look after your children's interests if you cannot.

You can feel confident about preparing your own will. For over 25 years Nolo has been the trusted name in do-it-yourself estate planning, and tens of thousands of people have made their own wills using Nolo resources. Following clear step-by-step instructions, you will prepare a will that leaves your property as you desire, provides for your minor children (if you have any), and names your executor—the person who will wrap up your estate when you die. After you prepare your final draft, sign your will, and have it witnessed, you can rest easy knowing that you've protected and provided for your loved ones.

Although most people will have no trouble making their own will with this book, it's not for everyone. For example, residents of Louisiana should not use this book. (These wills are legal for residents of every other state and Washington D.C.). Also, the wills in this book are basic legal documents that provide uncomplicated solutions to common estate planning concerns. If you are very wealthy, if you have complicated wishes for your property, or if you expect conflicts among your beneficiaries, then you should opt for more sophisticated estate planning and possibly a lawyer.

That said, for most people, these wills provide everything you need to leave your property, name your executor, and provide for your children—without the need for a lawyer. And when you're finished, peace of mind will reward your effort. Good luck!

CHAPTER

1

Making a Basic Will

This book is for people who want to make a basic will—nothing complex, no frills, just a valid will that does the job. It is for people who want to leave their property outright (no strings attached) when they die.

Following the step-by-step instructions in this book, you can create your own basic will that:

- leaves your property to the people and organizations you choose
- names someone to care for your minor children
- names someone to manage property you leave to minor children, including your own children, and
- names your executor, the person with authority to make sure that the terms of your will are carried out.

This book contains five sample will forms that are valid in every state and Washington D.C., with the exception of Louisiana (which has unique laws governing wills). These will forms have been carefully prepared to keep your work to a manageable amount.

Before you dive into making your will, first consider some preliminary will-making issues. First, is this the right will for you? The first section of this chapter will help you decide. Next, do you know the legal basics about making a will? Just to be sure, this chapter also gives you a quick tutorial of will law. Finally, how do you get started? The final sections of the chapter will show you how.

Is This Will Right for You?

The will in this book is simply perfect for many people, but not for everyone. Whether or not this basic will is right for you depends on the size of your estate, the complexity of your family situation, and your estate planning needs. This section will help you decide whether or not this will is right for your situation.

Using a Basic Will

Wills come in varying sizes and complexities. If you have a large estate and complicated wishes for your property, you might pay hundreds or thousands of dollars for a 50-page will drafted by lawyer. But if you have an average-sized estate (less than $1 million) and a simple plan for the distribution of your property, you may only need a four-page basic will that you can make yourself. This book shows you how to make that kind of basic will.

In fact, if you're healthy, relatively young, and own property less than the threshold limit for federal estate taxes (see Chapter 6), a basic will may be the only estate planning you need, at least for now. As you become older or wealthier, a basic will may no longer be the most economical and efficient method for passing your property. At that time, you will benefit from more sophisticated estate planning.

However, for now, if you have an average-sized estate and your plans for your property are fairly simple, a basic will document will work for you.

Living Overseas

You do not have to live in the U.S. to prepare a will that is valid in this country. To prepare a valid will if you live abroad, you must follow the formal will requirements presented in this book and maintain legal residence in a U.S. state. If you live overseas temporarily because you are in the armed services, your residence is the home of record you declared to the military authorities.

If you live overseas for business, education, or for the fun of it, you probably still have sufficient ties with a U.S. state to make it your legal home ("domicile" in legalese). For example, if you were born in New York, lived in New York, and are registered to vote there, then your residence is New York, for will-making purposes.

CAUTION

If your choice is not clear. If you do not maintain continuous ties with a particular state, or if you have homes in the U.S. and another country, consult a lawyer before preparing your will.

Making Your Own Will

Let me reassure you here at the start that preparing a basic will is not hard for most people. A basic will is a simple document used to transfer your own property to whomever you want to get it after you die. If you have a modest estate and simple wishes about what you want to do with it, you can make your own basic will.

Take a common situation, where both members of a married couple want to leave their property to the other spouse. If that spouse isn't alive, then all property is to be divided equally between their kids. What the couple wants can be said in two sentences. Why should accomplishing their straightforward desire in a valid legal document be so difficult that an expert must be paid? This book is based on the truth that there's no reason to involve a costly expert if a will writer has a simple estate and uncomplicated desires for what happens to that estate after they die.

Now let's look at a few real-life situations where a basic will from this book will work fine.

EXAMPLE 1:

Nyrit and Jerome, in their late 30s, own a home, two cars, and some savings. Their net estate totals $463,000. They have one child, Mark, age 12. Each prepares a will leaving all of his or her property to the other. If they die together, Mark is to receive all their property. Nyrit and Jerome agree that Nyrit's brother Iraz will care for Mark and manage the property until Mark turns 18.

EXAMPLE 2:

Sam, a widower, owns property with a net worth of $510,000. He has three adult children. He creates a will leaving all his property equally to his children. He specifies that if any child dies before him, that child's share is to be divided equally between the surviving children.

EXAMPLE 3:

Barbara is a divorced mother with two teenaged children and an estate totalling $123,000. Her ex-husband is a good father to their children, but is not good with money. Barbara prepares a will leaving all her property equally to her children. Because Barbara does not want her husband managing money she leaves to her children, she uses her will to appoint her sister Debbie to manage each child's property until each child turns 18.

Who Should Not Use This Book

If you have any complexities in your family situation, your property, or your beneficiary plans, this book is not for you. I could go on for pages trying to define what "complexities" are, but I believe I can rely on readers' common sense here. I'll offer a few specific examples of situations where you'd need to consult a lawyer to safely prepare your will:

- A child or family member has a disability or other special needs that you wish to address in your will when leaving that person property.

RESOURCE

Trusts for disabled children. Many Americans have a child or other loved one with a disability who requires long-term support and medical assistance from government programs. Money and property left directly to people with disabilities may disqualify them from government assistance. *Special Needs Trusts: Protect Your Child's Financial Future,* by Stephen Elias (Nolo), provides a solution. Using the book's clear-English explanations, information, instructions, and forms, you can create a special needs trust to provide for your loved one without jeopardizing public benefits.

- You are in a second or subsequent marriage, you have children from a prior marriage, and you believe there is a real potential for conflict between those children and the children you have with your current spouse. By contrast, there are certainly many second/subsequent marriages where such conflicts are unlikely. In that case, you can safely use a will from this book if it fits your other needs.
- You believe that someone might contest your will. To contest a will, the person contesting must argue that the will writer was not mentally competent when writing it, or that the will was procured by fraud or duress (such as some evildoer exerting undue influence over the will writer). I want to assure you that will contests are quite rare, and it's even more rare that anyone succeeds in overturning a will. Happily, the great majority of people don't face any realistic possibility of someone contesting their will.
- You want to create a trust protecting property for two generations. For example, you want to leave some property in trust for your child, and you also want that property to go to that child's children (your grandchildren) when your child dies.

See Chapter 11 for information about other Nolo self-help resources that address concerns not covered by this book.

Wills 101

There are surprisingly few legal restrictions and requirements in the will-making process. Let's look at the basic rules.

Who Can Make a Will?

You can create a valid will as long as you meet the following two criteria:

You must be at least 18 years of age. Some states allow younger people to make a will if they are married, in the military, or legally emancipated (have achieved adult status by order of a court).

You must be "of sound mind." This means you must:

- know what a will is, what it does, and that you are making one
- understand the relationship between yourself and those you would normally provide for in your will, such as a spouse or children, and
- understand the kind and quantity of property you own and how to distribute it.

In real-world terms, a person must be pretty far gone before his or her will could be invalidated by a judge on grounds of the will writer's state of mind. Forgetfulness, or some diminution of

Will-Writing Terms Defined

In discussing wills, I've tried to reduce legal jargon to a minimum. There are a few words or concepts you'll need to understand (but probably many fewer than you feared).

Beneficiaries or Primary Beneficiaries. These are the people or institutions you choose to leave some or all of your property to. People preparing a basic will usually are clear on who their beneficiaries are: a spouse or mate, children, and perhaps a few friends or charities.

Alternate Beneficiaries. These are the people or institutions you name to receive your property if your primary beneficiary dies before you.

Property. Everything you own. This can range from real estate ("real property" in legalese) to stocks, jewelry, cars, collectibles, clothes, and every other item you own.

Gifts. Throughout this book, the word "gift" or "gifts" is used to refer to property you leave through your will. Sometimes lawyers distinguish between "devises," which are gifts of real estate, and "bequests," which are gifts of any other kind of property. I'm happy to avoid this legalese by the use of the direct, and accurate, word "gift." In a different context, the word "gift" can also be used to refer to property freely transferred while all involved are living—from a small holiday gift to a substantial gift of cash.

Executor. This is the person you name to have authority to carry out the terms of your will. In some states, this person is also called your "personal representative" or "administrator."

Estate Planning. This term covers several different concerns. First is arranging for the transfer of your property, after your death, in the most economical and efficient manner. Such planning requires time and money—perhaps a substantial amount of money if you are wealthy or have complex wishes for leaving your property. Estate planning also includes providing for minor children (see Chapter 4), saving on estate taxes (if any), and arranging for the handling of your personal and financial affairs if you become incapacitated (see Chapter 6).

memory capacity, isn't sufficient to invalidate a will. If you can read and understand this book, your mind is sound enough to prepare a valid will.

Will Requirements

The laws in each state control whether a will made by a resident of that state is valid. You should make your will in the state where you live. If you move to another state, don't worry. A will that is valid in the state where it was made is also valid in all other states.

If you're temporarily living outside the United States, your state is where you have your permanent residence (or "state of record," if in the military). If you are living outside the United States permanently, do not use this book.

Following are the bare bones legal requirements of a valid will. The will must:

- include at least one substantive provision—either giving away some property or naming a guardian to care for minor children who are left without parents
- be signed and dated by the person making it, and
- be witnessed by two people who are not named as beneficiaries under the will.

Also strongly advisable is that the will:

- name someone to enforce the terms of the will (your executor), and
- be comprehensible; nonsensical, legal-sounding language, such as "I hereby give, bequeath and devise," is not necessary.

Contrary to what some people believe, a will need not be notarized to be legally valid.

Identifying Your State

Your state's laws affect a number of will-related issues, including probate procedures, marital property ownership, and state inheritance taxes. Most people are clear about which state they reside in. However, if you live in two or more states throughout the year, choose the state in which you are the most rooted as your state of residence. For instance, choose the state where you:

- are registered to vote
- register your motor vehicles
- own real estate or other valuable property, or
- maintain a business.

Types of Wills

Formal wills are typewritten, signed, and witnessed. That is the kind of will you would get from a lawyer, and that's the kind of will you can make using the forms from this book. There are a few other types of wills, but none are as legally reliable as a formal will.

Unwitnessed, handwritten wills—in legalese, "holographic wills"—are legally valid in only a few states. Further, handwritten wills are risky, even where legal. Most obviously, after your death, it may be difficult to prove that an unwitnessed, handwritten document was actually written by you and that you intended it to be your will. Further, many judges hold handwritten wills to very strict standards.

A typed will that has been properly signed and witnessed is much less vulnerable to a challenge of forgery or fabrication than a handwritten will. If need be, witnesses can later testify in court that the person whose name is on the will is the same person who signed it, and that the person made the will voluntarily and knowingly. Also, in many states a simple legal document called a self-proving affidavit may be signed by the will writer and the witnesses before a notary to make the will accepted in court more easily.

A few states accept the historical leftover of oral (spoken) wills, but only under very limited circumstances, such as when a mortally wounded soldier utters last wishes. Oral wills, even in the states that accept them, are of no use for people in normal life situations who don't fit into the narrow categories permitted.

Nevada is the only state to authorize an "electronic will"—that is, a will created and stored exclusively in an electronic format, usually on a computer. The will must use advanced technology to create a distinctive electronic signature and at least one other way to positively identify the will maker, such as retinal scan or voice or face recognition technology. While such technology may develop soon, no readily available methods currently exist for making an electronic will that is trustworthy and valid. It seems that Nevada wants to be legally prepared if such methods become available. If they do, other states are likely to follow Nevada's lead and allow electronic wills.

Finally, you may have heard of audiovisual wills, in which you are filmed (videotaped) as you speak your will desires. Audiovisual wills are not legally valid wills, because no state legislature has authorized them.

About Probate and Taxes

You've probably heard of probate and know it has a dubious reputation. In probate, the will of a person who died is filed with a court, and property is located and gathered by the estate's executor. Debts and taxes are paid, and the remaining property is distributed as the will directs. Most property passed by will must go through probate.

Probate certainly has drawbacks. It can be lengthy, commonly taking a year or more. It can also be expensive, normally requiring the services of lawyers and perhaps other specialists. Fees for these experts vary by state; however, payment will always come out of property you intended for family and friends.

The good news is that people whose situations warrant a basic will don't need to worry about probate at the time they write their will. The main concern of those who need a basic will is to make legal arrangements for the unlikely event that they die suddenly and unexpectedly. Yes, with a will there is a risk that their property may end up in probate. But for those who don't expect to die soon, or die wealthy, that risk is preferable to creating complex and often costly estate plans many years or decades before they're likely to come into play. (See Chapter 6 for more about probate and common ways to avoid it.)

Similarly, if a basic will is right for you, you probably don't have to worry about estate taxes either. Theoretically, the estate of every person who dies is subject to federal estate taxes. However, the personal estate tax exemption allows a set dollar amount of property to be transferred free of tax—the result is that only the estates of the wealthy end up actually owing federal estate tax.

The personal estate tax exemption varies by the year of death. In 2008, the exemption is $2 million and then it rises to $3.5 million in 2009. Under current law, there is no estate tax in 2010, but it reappears with an exemption of $1 million in 2011. Unless you own property worth more than the estate tax exemption for the year you die, your estate will not owe federal estate tax. For more about estate taxes, see Chapter 6.

CAUTION

People with estates above the estate tax threshold should consider estate planning beyond the scope of this book. If your property, whether individually or combined as a couple, exceeds the estate tax threshold, you may be able to save large amounts of money from the tax man by using more sophisticated planning methods than preparing a basic will. The rudiments of estate tax planning are discussed in Chapter 6.

Getting It Done

In the face of the intense emotional force and mystery of death, preparing a will may seem trivial. Although this is not a philosophical or spiritual book, I want to acknowledge that the emotional realities involved in a death are profound. But however one chooses to deal with death spiritually or philosophically, there are practical issues that must be confronted. A will is the easiest way to handle one of the most important practical matters: transferring property.

It's also important to acknowledge that the process of writing a will is more than a practical necessity. Deciding who you want to receive your property after your death can be a significant process. The peace of mind one achieves by preparing a will—having one thing on that nagging list of "really should be dones" behind you—is very real and satisfying. Certainly it's no denigration of death, or life, for you to be concerned with the wisest and most desirable distribution of your property.

In spite of this, the unfortunate reality is that many Americans still don't have a will. Why not? No one knows for sure, but here are my hunches:

- **Lack of reliable information.** The legal establishment has managed to mystify the process of writing a will. People fear either making mistakes by doing it themselves or they don't know they can prepare their own will. In fact, no law requires that a will be drafted or approved by a lawyer.
- **Cost.** People understandably resist paying a hunk of money to a lawyer for what their intuition tells them shouldn't be a difficult or complicated task.

- **Superstition.** Some people fear that just thinking about the practical consequences of one's death could somehow hasten death's arrival. We know better, right?
- **Good old procrastination.** For anyone with loved ones, it's certainly a bad idea to risk dying without a will, which leaves the distribution of one's estate for state law to determine. (This is called "dying intestate.")

What Happens If You Die Without a Will?

If you die without a valid will (or other valid property transfer device), your state law specifies who gets your property. All state laws divide a person's property among close family members. No flexibility is allowed. Perhaps worse, the court will appoint the person who will supervise the distribution of your property (and receive a fee from that property for services)—it won't be someone you've chosen. Also, if you have minor children and the other parent isn't involved, a court would appoint a guardian for your children without your input. Certainly, there have been instances where such a person was far more concerned with extracting hefty fees from the property than with the children's well-being. Enough said?

How to Proceed

This book is designed to lead you, sequentially, through the steps you'll need to take to prepare your own will. Chapters 2 through 5 discuss the heart of making a will: who gets what, what will happen to your children, who will you name to be your executor. Chapter 6 briefly looks beyond a basic will into general estate planning.

Chapter 7 contains detailed step-by-step instructions for completing each of the five sample will forms contained in Appendix B and on the CD-ROM. Depending on your marital status and whether or not you have children, you'll select the will form that's appropriate for you and carefully prepare a rough draft.

In Chapter 8, you'll learn how to use your completed will draft to create the final version of your will. Continuing to follow the instructions in Chapter 8, you'll sign and have your will witnessed, which completes the will-making process.

Chapters 9 and 10 cover what happens after you've made a will, including suggestions on storing your will and the possibility of making changes to it. Finally, Chapter 11 gives information about going beyond this book, by either using other Nolo resources or hiring a lawyer.

This Book at a Glance	
Here's a quick look at where you'll find what's in this book:	
Chapters 2–5	Helps you make decisions about your property, your children, and your executor.
Chapter 6	Provides general estate planning information.
Chapter 7	Describes how to make a first draft of your will, detailed section by section.
Chapter 8	Instructs how to prepare the final copy of your will, including how to sign it and have it witnessed.
Chapters 9–10	Tells you what to do with your will after it's done and when to revise it.
Chapter 11	Offers information about more complex estate planning and discusses when you might want to hire a lawyer.

CHAPTER

2

Your Beneficiaries

Your beneficiaries consist of any people or organizations you choose to receive your property after you die.

In this chapter, I address certain basic issues and concerns that may arise even if your beneficiary situation seems clear to you at first glance.

Categories of Beneficiaries

For will purposes, there are four categories of beneficiaries: primary beneficiaries, alternate beneficiaries, the residuary beneficiaries, and alternate residuary beneficiaries. Let's look at each of these in some detail.

Primary Beneficiaries

Your first choices to receive specific gifts of property are your primary beneficiaries. If you leave all your property to one person, that person is your only primary beneficiary. If you leave property to different people or organizations, you have several primary beneficiaries.

EXAMPLE:

Ken wants to leave several specific gifts. He wants to leave his house, car, and bank accounts to his wife, Gertrude. He wants to leave his art collection to the local museum. He wants to leave his books to the public library. Finally, he wants his daughter, Leslie, to inherit 60% of his vacation home and his son, Peter, to inherit 40%. All of these people and organizations are Ken's primary beneficiaries.

Alternate Beneficiaries

Many people are concerned about what would happen if a primary beneficiary dies before they do. Should you address this contingency in your will? For most people, the answer is "yes." You can name alternate beneficiaries to receive gifts if their first choice for that gift dies before (or around the same time) you do. Doing this is sensible for a number of reasons. Perhaps you've made some gifts to older people, or relatives in poor health who may not survive you. Or maybe you just don't want to worry about redoing your will if a beneficiary dies before you.

EXAMPLE:

Juanita leaves most of her property to her husband, Alfredo. She leaves some jewelry to her sister, Isabella. She names her son, Macito, as the alternate beneficiary for the property left to her husband. She names Isabella's daughter, Simone, as an alternate beneficiary for the jewelry.

On the other hand, some people aren't concerned about their beneficiaries dying before they do and decide not to name alternate beneficiaries. This approach is more likely when the primary beneficiaries are considerably younger than the will writer. Also, many people figure that if a beneficiary does die before they do, they'll probably have time enough to modify their will to name a new beneficiary. If you don't name an alternate beneficiary, and the beneficiary fails to survive you, the gift will become part of your residuary estate, as discussed below.

Charities as Beneficiaries

You may want to leave property to a charity or a public or private organization—for example, the United Way, the Greenview Battered Women's Shelter, the University of Maine.

The organization you name need not be set up as a nonprofit, unless you wish your estate to qualify for a charitable estate tax deduction—although few readers of a basic will book need to be concerned with that. In fact, you can leave property to any organization you consider worthy. The only limitation is that the organization must not be set up for some illicit or illegal purpose.

On balance, I urge you to name alternate beneficiaries. It's easy to do; Chapter 7 will take you through that process. Therefore, if the unexpected occurs and a beneficiary does not survive you, you'll have your will distribution plan intact.

Residuary Beneficiaries

Your residuary estate consists of all property you own at your death, except for:

- property you've specifically identified in your will that passes to primary and alternate beneficiaries you've named, and
- property that passes to people outside of your will because of other arrangements you made while you were alive, such as putting the property in a living trust, setting up a pay-on-death bank account, or creating a joint tenancy ownership in the property. (I discuss these arrangements in Chapter 6.)

Your residuary estate includes property you overlooked when you made your will, as well as property you acquired after you made your will.

You can, if you wish, name one sole residuary beneficiary or any number of residuary beneficiaries, possibly combining individuals and organizations, to share in your residuary estate.

How an individual will writer decides to distribute his or her property can vary widely. Some people leave the bulk, or even all, of their property to residuary beneficiaries. Some name specific beneficiaries for many, or even all, of their specific items of property. And, of course, there is a broad range where these two approaches are blended to suit individual needs.

Alternate Residuary Beneficiaries

Your alternate residuary beneficiary or beneficiaries are whoever you name to receive your residuary estate if the residuary beneficiary (or beneficiaries) dies before you do.

EXAMPLE:

Barbara makes specific gifts of cash to each of her two children. She leaves the remainder of her property—her residuary estate—to her husband, Paul. She names her children as the alternate residuary beneficiaries, to inherit in equal shares. When Barbara dies, Paul will receive everything she owns, with the exception of the money left to her children. But if Paul doesn't outlive Barbara, the children will receive their specified cash gifts plus equal shares of the residuary estate.

Shared Gifts

Many people understandably want to leave one or more items of property to be shared by more than one beneficiary. An obvious example is a parent who wants to leave all her property in equal shares to her five children. Another example is someone who wants to leave 75% of his house to his sister and 25% to his nephew. At first this may seem straightforward, but there can be lurking complexities with shared gifts.

Shared Gifts to Primary or Residuary Beneficiaries

The major issue here is how to clearly specify what rights each beneficiary has in the gift. The wills in this book state that if you don't specify shares (percentages), all beneficiaries of a shared gift receive an equal share.

If you want to give unequal shares, specify that by percentage amounts. Percentages work better than dollar amounts because they are not affected by fluctuations in the value of the gift property. By contrast, if your stock account has a current value of $100,000 and you leave $40,000 worth of the account to Suzy and $60,000 to Myron, there's going to be confusion, and probably trouble, if the account value has fallen to $77,000 when you die. To avoid this, identify the shares in any gift or in your residuary estate by percentages. And, of course, make sure the percentages you leave add up to 100%.

EXAMPLE:

Mariko wants to leave several shared gifts. She leaves an unimproved parcel of land to her sons, Kai and Toshiro, in equal shares. She leaves her art collection divided by market value to her siblings: 50% to her brother, Chiyuki, 30% to her sister Yukiko, and 20% to her other sister Noriko. Finally, she leaves her stock portfolio to her three nephews: 50% to Kunio, 30% to Iwao, and 20% to Eiji.

Shared gifts can raise serious problems, even conflicts, about control. Suppose your house passes in equal shares to your three children. What happens if two want to sell it and one doesn't? Or take the art collection in the previous example that Mariko left to her siblings divided 50%, 30%, and 20%. How are the values of these shares to be determined? If all three siblings agree to sell the art collection and they can find buyers, there shouldn't be a problem. But suppose they want to keep their portions. How do they agree on what is 20% of the value of the art collection? Or 30%? Or 50%? Must they hire an appraiser? Will one appraiser be enough? And what if they all want the same artwork?

This book takes a very simple approach to questions of conflict between shared gifts. The wills in this book say that all shared gifts must be sold, and the net proceeds distributed as the will directs, unless all beneficiaries for that gift agree in writing, after the will writer's death, that the gift need not be sold. If all beneficiaries agree to retain the property, they must find a mutually agreeable method for resolving valuation issues and any other potential conflicts.

SEE AN EXPERT

If you want to allow one of the beneficiaries to prevent the sale of a shared gift. With a lawyer's help, you can add provisions to your will to address control over shared gifts. For instance, "The house cannot be sold unless all three of my children agree on it." But often, other problems result from these types of provisions. If two want to sell the house, but one doesn't, who has to manage the house? Does the house have to be rented at market value? Can the child who wants to keep the house live in it? If she does, must she pay the others any rent? What happens if one child dies? Clearly, trying to address these contingencies in a will removes it from the "basic" category. Figuring out sensible ways to write a will covering these "what ifs" is a lawyer's stock and trade. But before you pay an attorney to do this, be clear you really feel it is necessary for you to resolve such questions. For many people, it makes more sense to leave shared gifts outright to the beneficiaries. If all beneficiaries agree to keep it, fine. If not, selling the property and dividing the proceeds as you've directed in your will is the direct and clear solution.

Alternate Beneficiaries and Alternate Residuary Beneficiaries for Shared Gifts

Let's say you leave shared gifts, and one of the beneficiaries dies before you. Who receives the gift (assuming you didn't redo your will)? You have two options:

- you can have the surviving primary or residuary beneficiaries share the interest of any beneficiary who dies, or
- you can use your will to name one or more alternate beneficiaries for each primary or residuary beneficiary of the shared gift.

If you choose the first option (having the gift divided among surviving beneficiaries), you don't need to do anything to a will prepared from this book. All the book's will forms state that: "A deceased beneficiary's share of a shared (or residuary) gift shall be divided equally among the surviving beneficiaries of that gift, unless this will specifically provides otherwise."

EXAMPLE:

John leaves a specific gift of land to be shared equally by Tony, Melinda, and Biff. Tony predeceases John. When John dies, the gift will be divided equally between Melinda and Biff (unless John revised his will after Tony died).

If you want to specify who the alternate beneficiaries should be for each primary or residuary beneficiary of a shared gift, you must simply split the shared gift in separate portions so that you can make separate specific gifts to different beneficiaries. Then name different alternate beneficiaries for each primary or residuary beneficiary.

EXAMPLE:

Mike wants to leave his house to his two sons, Anthony and Travis, and his sister, Virginia. He wants each son to receive a 40% share and his sister a 20% share of the house. In the event one son does not survive him, he wants that son's share to go that son's child or children. If his sister predeceases him, Mike wants that 20% share to pass to Virginia's son, Malcolm. To accomplish his goals, Mike makes three separate specific gifts in his will, divided as follows:

40% share in house:	Primary beneficiary—Anthony Alternate beneficiary—Anthony's children, Jessica and Tricia, equally
40% share in house:	Primary beneficiary—Travis Alternate beneficiary—Travis's son, Jason
20% share in house:	Primary beneficiary— Virginia Alternate beneficiary—Virginia's son, Malcolm

Survivorship Period

In will terms, a "survivorship period" is a defined period of time by which a beneficiary must outlive the will writer in order to legally receive property left to that beneficiary. If that beneficiary fails to survive the will writer by the set time period, the property goes to the next in line to receive it, as specified in the will.

Without a survivorship period, a beneficiary who dies shortly after you never actually receives your intended gift; instead, it becomes part of his or her estate. The result is that the property you'd left for a loved one to use and enjoy merely raises the dollar value of the recipient's estate, possibly becoming subject to additional probate fees. Also, this property now passes under the terms of your beneficiary's will, rather than going to someone you've chosen.

The wills in this book impose a 45-day survivorship period on all gifts left to beneficiaries, primary, residuary, or alternate.

EXAMPLE:

Using a will from this book, Justine leaves her jewelry to her sister Edina. The alternate beneficiary is Justine's niece, Muriel. Justine dies; Edina dies 32 days later. Justine's jewelry goes to Muriel, because Edina didn't survive Justine by 45 days. The jewelry was never legally owned by Edina.

Why do the wills in this book impose a 45-day survivorship period, as opposed to, say, 90 days or nine days? Nolo has chosen 45 days as a sensible balance between a period that lasts for many months, needlessly tying up the estate, and one that seems too short to be useful.

Simultaneous Death

Many couples, married or not, are concerned about what would happen in the unlikely event that they both die at or near the same time. The possibility may be remote, but it's surely been known to happen. For example, what happens if the couple dies together in an airplane crash, a fatal car accident or a hiking disaster? This book's will forms provide clauses that make clear who will receive gifts from each person's estate in such a tragedy.

Couples are often concerned that one spouse may briefly outlive the other, sending all the deceased spouse's property in the estate of the (briefly) surviving spouse. This can be undesirable for estate tax reasons, and also may result in a property distribution the first spouse didn't want. After all, there are no laws requiring each spouse to choose all the same beneficiaries.

The 45-day survivorship periods described above are applicable to all beneficiaries, including a spouse or partner. Therefore, one spouse simply cannot inherit the other spouse's property if the survivor only lives a few minutes or for any period less than 45 days beyond the death of the first spouse.

EXAMPLE:

Pete and Margaret each leave all their property to each other as residuary beneficiaries but have different choices for alternate residuary beneficiaries. The couple takes a ride in a hot air balloon, which explodes. Pete dies almost instantly; Margaret lingers alive for five days, then dies. Because of the 45-day survivorship period, Margaret never legally inherits Pete's property. Pete's property goes to his alternate residuary beneficiaries. Margaret's property goes to her alternate residuary beneficiaries.

Imposing Limits on Your Gifts

You cannot use a will from this book to impose limits or restrictions on your gifts (aside from controls over gifts to minor children, discussed in Chapter 4). Limits or restrictions are any conditions or "strings" attached to the gift, such as:

- your house will go your sister after you die, and then to your children after her death
- your son is to receive money if he goes to college, or
- your vintage Barbie doll collection will go to your best friend if the dolls are in good condition. (Who is to determine if the dolls are in good condition?)

In some situations, there can be very sensible reasons for a person to want to impose limits or restrictions on a gift, but those complexities are beyond the scope of this book. Here are two common examples.

EXAMPLE 1:

Eleanor, in her 50s, is in her second marriage. She has three children from her prior marriage. Her major asset is a house that she owns (the mortgage is paid off). If she dies before her husband, Peter, she wants him to be able to continue living in the house. But when he dies, she wants the house's worth to be divided equally among her three children. In this situation, Eleanor would want to create, and have her lawyer draft, what's called a "life estate" trust, allowing Peter the right to live in the house for his life, but no rights to own the house or leave it to others in his will. After Peter's death, the house would pass to Eleanor's children.

EXAMPLE 2:

Joe and LaToya have a mentally disabled son, Lamont, age 24. They each want to leave money for Lamont's benefit, but he cannot manage money himself. After both spouses die, there must be a trustee of a trust created by Joe and LaToya to manage property left for Lamont's benefit. This trust should be prepared to minimize the possibility that the principal could be consumed by a government agency in recompense for government aid Lamont receives. This type of trust is called a "special needs" trust. See *Special Needs Trusts: Protect Your Child's Financial Future*, by Stephen Elias (Nolo).

SEE AN EXPERT

Restrictions always raise complexities. There are many more reasons why someone might sensibly want to impose restrictions on a gift. My point here is simply that you can't impose any restrictions using a will from this book (beyond those imposed by the form itself, such as the 45-day survivorship period or special property provisions for minor children). You should see an attorney before imposing any restrictions on a gift.

Disinheritance

Disinheritance is not a subject that typically concerns most people preparing a basic will. The word "disinheritance" has harsh, perhaps sad, overtones, because it means you've decided to exclude from your will someone very close to you, generally a family member. But sad or not, it's certainly been known to happen. Here are the state law rules and limits regarding disinheritance.

Spouses

In the majority of states, called "common law states," you do not have the legal right to disinherit your spouse. (See Chapter 3.) In these states, to be safe, you must leave your spouse at least one-half of your estate.

The other states are "community property states," where you own half of the community property owned by you and your spouse. You can leave your half of the community property (as well as any separate property you own) to anyone you wish. A spouse in these states has no legal right to any of your property when you die.

Children

In all states, you can disinherit a child, but your intent to do so must be clearly expressed in your will. The same functional result can be accomplished by leaving the child a very small amount of property. But you cannot disinherit a child simply by failing to mention that child in your will. If you don't mention a child in your will, that child generally has a legal right to some of your property. (The rules for disinheriting a child are discussed in more detail in Chapter 4.)

Disinheriting Other People

With the exception of spouses and children not expressly disinherited in your will, you can disinherit anyone else you want to by simply not naming them in the will. Actually, the word "disinherit" isn't really correct here, because no one other than a spouse and children has any legal right to your property (unless you've made a valid contract to leave someone some property in your will). So omitting any other person from your will isn't disinheriting that person, because they weren't entitled to inherit in the first place.

You may have heard that some lawyers recommend leaving $1 to relatives or friends you want to disinherit. Doing this is not legally necessary, and there's no sensible reason to do it. Why mention a relative or friend in your will only to leave them $1, when they otherwise wouldn't be entitled to anything? Tracking down such beneficiaries just to hand over one buck can be a real hassle for your executor.

SEE AN EXPERT

If you think someone might contest your will. If you suspect that after your death, one of your relatives might contest your will, see a lawyer. Doing so will help ensure that you've done all you can to discourage a will contest and that your intentions will prevail if a contest does occur.

If You Want to Explain Your Decisions

The wills in this book have been designed to allow you to make a legal and unambiguous will. They do not contain space for you to explain to your beneficiaries why you made your gifts, or to express other sentiments and emotions.

Fortunately, there is a way you can have your final say about personal matters without risking your will's legal validity or integrity. You can write a letter to accompany your will expressing your thoughts to those who survive you. Your letter must expressly state that you do not intend the letter to modify or affect your will in any way, and that you know the letter is solely a personal statement of your feelings and emotions.

Writing a letter to your loved ones to explain why you wrote your will as you did—and knowing they will read your reasoning after your death—can give you some peace of mind during life about your property distribution. (Writing this type of letter is explained further in Chapter 8.) ●

CHAPTER

3

Property Ownership

As you know, you use a will to leave your property to others after your death. Obviously, you can't leave property by will unless it belongs to you in the first place. Many people won't have any real questions about property ownership. "Hey, I [or my spouse and I] own a house, household furnishings, clothes, a car, a checking account, a small retirement account, and a smaller savings account—what else do I need to know?" In this instance, nothing at all. For people with small estates, or those who keep their property information in their heads, knowing what property they own is easy.

Further, if you plan to leave all of your property to one person or as a shared gift to two or more persons, you don't need a detailed list of all of your property, no matter how complicated your holdings. Similarly, if you plan to make only one, or few, individual gifts and leave the rest of your property to one person, you shouldn't need to spend a lot of time cataloging what you own.

However, many people do need to take a deeper look at their property issues, especially if they co-own property with anyone, including a spouse. Some readers may be surprised to find that they don't own what they think they do. Most will learn they have no problem at all here. But do read on, because you need to be clear about your property situation to create a will using this book.

This chapter helps you:

- learn some basic legal rules about property ownership so that you can make sure you own the property you believe you do, and
- inventory your property, if you need to.

Definition of "Property"

I have already defined property (in Chapter 1) as being anything you own. Lawyers make various distinctions between types of property. "Real property" means real estate, land, and any buildings permanently attached to that land. "Personal property" means all other types of property, from a tube of lipstick to hundreds of thousands of dollars in a stock investment.

Happily for your will-writing purposes, you don't need to bother with different classifications of property. Any item you own is your property. It may have market value, such as a house or car, or it may have none, such as family photos or treasured family letters. It's all your property, and you may distribute each item as you wish.

Basic Rules for Giving Away Property

Here I cover some basic rules about leaving property by will that people sometimes have questions about.

Rule 1: Your State's Laws Govern All or Most of Your Property

Generally, the laws of the state where you legally reside apply to all property you own. If you are married, this can be extremely important, because state laws in most states give your spouse certain rights to your property, no matter what you provide in your will. Otherwise, state laws normally have no impact on will distribution. However, in certain instances, laws of another state or country apply:

- **Real estate located in another state.** Each state's laws govern all real estate located within that state.
- **Property located in another country.** Each country has its own laws governing all property (real estate, bank accounts, and all other items) that exists within its borders.

The state of your legal residence (where you legally live) is where you make your home. You can have only one legal residence. If you divide up the year by living in two or more states or you are temporarily residing outside the United States, choose as your state of residence the state in which you are the most rooted—for instance, where you:

- are registered to vote
- register your motor vehicles
- own real estate or other valuable property
- have checking, savings, and other investment accounts, or
- maintain a business.

If you live overseas temporarily because you are in the armed services, your residence will be the home of record you declared to the military authorities. See "Living Overseas" in Chapter 1.

Rule 2: Only Property You Own at the Time of Death Is Passed by Will

Few people try to leave property they've never owned. Problems can arise, however, when a will writer leaves a specific item of property that was sold, given away, or lost between the time the will was drafted and the will writer's death. What happens in this case? That's easy: If a specific gift is made in a will, and that property is no longer owned by the will writer when he or she dies, the gift is void. That's it.

EXAMPLE:

Al has a classic MG convertible that he's lovingly (and expensively) restored and owned for decades. In his will, he specifically leaves the car to his daughter, Darlene. But several years after writing his will, Al experiences some tight financial times and sells the MG. When Al dies, Darlene obviously won't get the car. Further, she has no right to the dollar value of the car.

MORAL:

Be sure you keep your will up to date regarding your property. Note that if you leave all your property to one person, or divide it all among several, there's no specific gift that could be later voided, so there is far less chance of your beneficiaries feeling disappointed.

Rule 3: You Can't Use a Will to Give Away Property That Will Automatically Be Transferred Upon Your Death

It's common to arrange for some property to be passed automatically to others upon the owner's death, thereby avoiding probate. This property cannot be given away by will. For example, there are many specific kinds of property for which you can name beneficiaries on the ownership documents, including most individual retirement plans, such as IRAs, 401(k)s, and profit-sharing plans. (If you don't know what one, or all, of these are, don't worry. That means you don't have one.) You can also name beneficiaries on the ownership documents of insurance policies, certain types of bank accounts (called pay-on-death accounts) and securities (stocks and bonds) held under the Uniform Transfer-on-Death Security Act.

EXAMPLE:

Jordan takes out a life insurance policy and names his daughter, Carmel, as the beneficiary, to receive the proceeds when he dies. Carmel will receive the proceeds directly after Jordan dies; the money won't pass through Jordan's will or the probate court. Even if Jordan names different beneficiaries for the life insurance proceeds in his will, this designation would be meaningless and ineffective; Carmel will still get the money.

Other legal methods of transferring property at death include well-known probate avoidance methods such as living trusts and joint tenancy. All major transfer methods are discussed in Chapter 6.

Rule 4: You May Not Be Able to Give Away Co-Owned Business Property by Will

You need to check the ownership agreement of any shared business to see what your rights are to leave your interest by will. Often the other owners have the right to buy out a deceased owner's interest using a valuation method determined in the ownership agreement. Of course, even if the other owners have the option to buy out your share of the business, the agreement will rarely require them to do so.

EXAMPLE:

Lucy is partners with Arabella and Jane in a garden nursery business. Their partnership agreement states that if one partner wants to sell her interest in the business, the other two partners have the right to buy that interest, if they chose to. The agreement also defines a method for determining the price the two partners would pay for the other partner's interest.

Lucy cannot leave her share of the business by her will (unless the other partners agree to waive the conflicting clauses of the partnership agreement). However, Lucy could use her will to leave any money received from the sale of her partnership interest to a beneficiary she names.

If you can't leave your business interest, you can still leave whatever money the surviving owners pay for your share by your will, so that the money goes to whomever you want to receive it. Because you can't know in advance what the buyout price will be, don't leave specific dollar amounts to beneficiaries. You should simply leave all of your interest to one beneficiary, or percentages of your interest to different beneficiaries.

Rule 5: Property Loans and Encumbrances Become the Responsibility of the Beneficiaries

Using the wills in this book, property with money owed on it, such as a car with a loan on it or a house with a mortgage, will pass to your beneficiary subject to the encumbrance. In other words, if you don't own something free and clear, neither will your beneficiaries. If you want your estate to pay off the loan or mortgage, use another Nolo will-writing resource. (See Chapter 11.)

Rule 6: You Can't Leave Money or Property to Pets Outright

Pets aren't people (even if they sometimes act like they are), and they can't legally own money or property. That means you can't leave anything to them in your will. You also can't use your will to put binding requirements on your pet's care, such as requiring certain grooming procedures or a particular type of food. But you can use your will to be sure that, when you die, your pets will get good care and a good home. The easiest way to do this is to make an arrangement with a friend or family member to take care of your pet. Then, in your will, you leave your pet to that person, along with some money for the expense of your pet's feeding and care.

In an increasing number of states, you can establish a trust for your pet. The trust is a legally independent entity, managed by a trustee you name. You also define the terms of the trust—how your pet is to be cared for—in the trust document. Pet trusts can be desirable for people who feel they'd prefer not to leave their pet outright to someone. But creating a pet trust is more costly and complicated than simply leaving your pet outright.

States That Allow Trusts for Pets	
Alabama	Nevada
Alaska	New Hampshire
Arizona	New Jersey
Arkansas	New Mexico
California	New York
Colorado	North Carolina
District of Columbia	North Dakota
Florida	Ohio
Hawaii	Pennsylvania
Idaho	Rhode Island
Illinois	South Carolina
Indiana	South Dakota
Iowa	Tennessee
Kansas	Texas
Maine	Utah
Michigan	Virginia
Missouri	Washington
Montana	Wisconsin
Nebraska	Wyoming

SEE AN EXPERT

You'll need an attorney to prepare a pet trust. You cannot prepare a pet trust on your own. You'll need to hire an attorney to get the document drafted.

Taking Stock of Your Property

People who are preparing a basic will usually have a good idea of what they own, without needing to make an extensive property inventory. Many readers won't need to inventory their property at all, especially if they are leaving all of it to one or just a few persons. But before you prepare your will, it's wise to pause and check to be sure there are no special items of property you might have overlooked. This is particularly important if you want to leave some special or sentimental items to specific beneficiaries. For example, maybe you have a collection of special heirlooms you want to give to a family member or close friend. Nor is it just expensive items you may care the most about; certain photos, journals, or mementos of friendship may be equally precious.

It won't take much time for you to go through the "Property You May Want to Leave by Will" list on the next page to help jog your memory about what property you own.

RESOURCE

If your property ownership is complex and valuable. If you believe an in-depth inventory would be helpful, you should seek help beyond this book.

Property You May Want to Leave by Will

Real Estate (land and items permanently attached to land)

Agricultural land
Boat/marina dock space
Condo
Co-op
Duplex
House
Mobile home
Rental property
Timeshare
Undeveloped land
Vacation house

Personal Property (property other than real estate)

Animals
Antiques
Appliances
Art
Bank and cash accounts:
- Certificates of deposit
- Checking accounts
- Money market funds
- Savings accounts

Bicycles
Books
Business interests
Cameras, photographic and video equipment
China, crystal, silver
Clothing, furs
Coins, stamps
Collectibles (records, dolls, baseball cards, and so on)
Computer equipment
Copyrights, patents, trademarks
Electronic equipment
Family heirlooms
Furniture
Hobbies
Household furnishings
Inheritances
Jewelry
Letters, documents, papers
Medals, awards, trophies
Musical instruments
Pets
Photographs
Precious metals
Promissory notes, debts owed to you
Religious items, artifacts
Royalties
Safe deposit contents
Securities:
- Bonds
- Commodities
- Mutual funds
- Stocks

Sentimental items
Small businesses
Sports equipment
Tools
U.S. bills, notes, and bonds
Vehicles, boats, aircraft:
- Airplanes
- Automobiles
- Boats
- Motorcycles
- Motor homes/RVs

Watches
Wedding and engagement rings

The Beneficiary Worksheet

Once you've pinned down what property you own, you may find the Beneficiary Worksheet (in Appendix B and on the CD-ROM) helpful for deciding who gets what. You can use it to work out who your beneficiaries are and exactly what each one receives. The Beneficiary Worksheet can be useful in a variety of situations:

- Readers who simply aren't sure how they want to divide up their property can rough out (in pencil) their options and make decisions as they go along.
- The Beneficiary Worksheet can help you organize your will-writing choices so that you don't overlook important items of property or accidentally forget any beneficiaries.
- Some readers own a variety of property and wish to divide it among a number of people and organizations. The Beneficiary Worksheet can be a handy place for organizing that data.

Let me conclude by reminding you that many readers' situations are clear enough so that they'll have no need for the Beneficiary Worksheet. Don't use it if it isn't helpful.

You Don't Need to Use Legal Terminology to Leave Property by Will

Some people ask, "Don't I need to use some technical, legal language to describe property I leave in my will?" The answer is no. There are no legal requirements governing how you identify your property. I discuss this matter now, because I want to reassure you that when you're ready to prepare your will, you won't be burdened with legalese when it comes to describing your property. (This matter is further discussed in Chapter 7.)

Here's some more good news: If you leave all your property to one person (or all your property to multiple beneficiaries in a shared gift), you won't even have to bother describing it.

If you leave a number of items of property to one or several beneficiaries, that property must be described sufficiently so that those beneficiaries, and the person you've named to carry out your will, are clear about what you meant. All that is needed to achieve this is a plain, commonsense description of the property. Describing your property in your will won't be hard and is certainly no stumbling block to preparing your will yourself.

Types of Property Ownership

Here I briefly cover the basic legal forms of property ownership. This section should provide sufficient information to alert you if you may have a complicated property ownership situation. If you are married, you'll also need to read "Marital Property," below, which covers property rights between a husband and wife.

Outright Ownership

The simplest form of ownership exists when you are the only owner—that is, you do not share ownership and you are not married. For the purpose of making your will, you are the sole owner—even if a lender has some legal interest in the property until you pay off the loan, as is true with car notes and house mortgages.

Tenancy in Common

Tenancy in common is a form of shared ownership where the owners decide on each individual percentage of ownership. Ownership shares can be equal, but it is also possible to arrange for unequal shares by deed or written contract. Each co-owner has an equal right to use the property and is free to transfer, by will, his or her interest to anyone she or he chooses.

Tenancy in common is the most common way for unmarried people to own property together. Married couples also can use this form of co-ownership, but more often choose joint tenancy or tenancy by the entirety, discussed below.

Joint Tenancy With Right of Survivorship

Any two (or more) people can own property—typically real estate or a bank account—in joint tenancy with right of survivorship. When one of them dies, his or her share automatically goes to the surviving owner. *A joint tenant cannot use a will to leave his or her share of joint tenancy property to someone else.*

EXAMPLE:

Avram is a widower. He and his brother Sid own a house together. Avram wants to leave large gifts to his son, Ben, and his daughter, Freida. He plans to leave Ben a large gift of cash. At first, he considers leaving Freida his half of the house. Then Avram looks at the deed to the house and realizes that the property is held in joint tenancy, so Avram's brother automatically owns his half if Avram dies first. If Avram uses his will to leave his share of the house to Freida, she won't be entitled to it, meaning Ben would get cash and Freida would get nothing. Avram instead decides to leave both Ben and Freida cash gifts.

Simultaneous Death of Joint Tenants

If all joint tenants die simultaneously, no one owner has survived any of the others. In that case, each joint tenant's interest in the property passes by their will. Under the wills in this book, in this situation, a person's joint tenancy interest would become part of the residuary estate and pass to the named residuary beneficiary or alternate.

EXAMPLE: Sylvia and Henry are married and own their home in joint tenancy. They are both killed in a boating disaster. Sylvia's one-half interest in the joint tenancy property passes to her residuary beneficiary. Henry's one-half goes to his residuary beneficiary. (If Sylvia and Henry were the other's residuary beneficiary, each one's property would go to his or her alternate residuary beneficiary.)

Joint tenancies with right of survivorship are created by specific words in an ownership document, such as a real estate deed or bank account certificate. To find out whether you own property in joint tenancy, check the document for the words "joint tenants," "joint tenancy," or "with the right of survivorship." A few states require the document to read "joint tenancy with the right of survivorship." Oregon, for example, requires the words "tenancy in common with the right of survivorship" to set up this kind of joint ownership.

SEE AN EXPERT

See a lawyer if you're unsure how you own your property. If you're not clear about how you own your property, see a lawyer before you make your will. Otherwise you may try to use your will to leave property that isn't yours.

Sometimes owners decide to change ownership of property from joint tenancy to tenancy in common in order to leave their interests to someone other than the surviving joint tenant(s). In most all states, it's relatively easy for one owner to accomplish this change. Indeed, in most states, transfers out of joint tenancy into another form of co-ownership can be done even if the other joint tenant objects. You need to check with some authority, such as a title company or a real estate lawyer, to determine the precise mechanics required.

EXAMPLE:

Avram (from the previous example) decides he wants his share of his house to go to his daughter, and not to his brother Sid. Avram prepares the documents required in his state to take the house out of joint tenancy and place it in tenancy in common. Then he and Sid sign the documents. They each continue to own 50% of the house, but Avram may now leave his interest to his daughter, by will, without trouble.

Restrictions on Joint Tenancy in Alaska

In Alaska, joint tenancy is not allowed, except for a husband and wife who may own property together as tenants by the entirety.

Community Property With Right of Survivorship

Five states—Alaska, Arizona, California, Nevada, and Texas—expressly permit spouses to hold property "as community property with right of survivorship." In other words, in these states spouses can obtain the benefit of joint tenancy while owning community property. With this form of ownership, a surviving spouse automatically receives a deceased spouse's share of community property, outside of probate.

Tenancy by the Entirety

This form of ownership is basically the same as joint tenancy with right of survivorship discussed above but is limited to married couples. The phrase "tenancy by the entirety" or "as tenants by the entirety" must appear in the deed. When one spouse dies, the entire interest in the property automatically goes to the other. Before tenancy by the entirety property can be changed to some other form of property ownership, both spouses must agree to the change.

States with Tenancy by the Entirety Ownership

Alaska*	New Jersey
Arkansas	New York*
Delaware	North Carolina*
District of Columbia	Ohio (only if created before 4/4/85)
Florida*	Oklahoma
Hawaii	Oregon*
Illinois*	Pennsylvania
Indiana*	Rhode Island
Kentucky*	Tennessee
Maryland	Utah*
Massachusetts	Vermont
Michigan	Virginia
Mississippi	Wyoming
Missouri	

*Allows tenancy by the entirety only for real estate.

Marital Property

SKIP AHEAD

If you're not married. If you're single, divorced, or widowed, skip the rest of this chapter. But if you're married or in the process of getting a divorce, you'll need to read this section.

The great majority of married people leave all or most of their property to the surviving spouse at death. For them, the nuances of state marital property law are not relevant. Even if you want to leave some gifts to other family members, friends, or institutions, your marital property situation will usually be simple, as long as you're leaving at least one-half of your property to your spouse.

If you plan to leave substantial amounts to someone instead of, or in addition to, your spouse, the picture becomes more complicated. Questions of which spouse owns what property may then become important, unless your spouse consents to your plan for property disposition, as is most often true when older spouses leave property directly to their adult children.

In this section, I briefly cover the main issues of marital property. I don't go into these issues in depth, because few users of this book face such concerns. If after reading this section you think you may have a more complex marital partnership problem, turn to Chapter 11.

Fortunately, learning the basics of marital property law is not difficult. For the purpose of deciding what is in your estate when you die, states are divided into two types: community property states and common law property states.

Community Property States	Common Law Property States
Alaska*	All other states
Arizona	
California	
Idaho	
Nevada	
New Mexico	
Texas	
Washington	
Wisconsin**	

*Allows community property only by written agreement.
**While Wisconsin is not technically a community property state, its marital property law closely resembles those found in community property states. This law covers all property owned at a person's death.

Same-Sex Couples

The laws affecting same-sex couples vary by state. Some states do not legally recognize same-sex relationships at all, while other states offer a variety of rights to lesbian and gay couples.

Massachusetts is the only state that allows resident lesbian and gay couples to marry. The following states provide domestic partnership rights for registered couples: California, Connecticut, Hawaii, Maine, New Jersey, New Hampshire, Oregon, Vermont, and Washington. Each state's domestic partnership law provides registered couples with the same inheritance rights as are granted to married couples in that state.

However, even if you live in a state with a domestic partnership law, you should write your own will—do not rely on state law to distribute your property for you. State inheritance laws are very unlikely to coincide precisely with your own wishes. It is not wise to let your state decide how your property will be distributed after your death.

When you prepare your will with this book, select a form designed for a nonmarried person (even if you are legally married in Massachusetts). Use Form 3 or 4 if you want to make a will as a single person. Or use Form 5 if you want to name your partner under "Marital Status." If this does not feel right to you, or if you have any questions about your rights, you may want to talk with a lawyer in your state who is an expert in this field. Also, consider reading *A Legal Guide for Lesbian & Gay Couples*, by Denis Clifford, Frederick Hertz, and Emily Doskow (Nolo), which provides a gold mine of interesting and important information about the legal aspects of your same-sex relationship.

Your Marital Status and Your Will

Most readers' marital status is clear—they're married or they're not. But in some situations, a person's marital status, for will-writing purposes, isn't so clear. Your marital status could affect how and to whom you can leave your property. For example, if you're separated but not yet divorced, your estranged spouse may have a right to inherit one-third to one-half of what you own.

If you're in the process of divorcing, or are planning to marry, it's fine to make a will now. But make sure you write your will over again after your marital status changes. (See Chapter 10.)

If you are unsure whether you are married or single according to law, here are some tips:

- **Separation, or pending divorce or annulment.** You remain legally married until a court issues a formal decree of divorce or annulment, signed by a judge. This is true even if you and your spouse have filed for divorce or annulment, are legally separated as declared in a legal document, or live apart for an extended time.
- **Common law marriages.** In a number of states, an unmarried woman and man automatically become legally married if they live together and either hold themselves out to the public as being married or actually intend to be married to one another. Common law marriages are recognized in Alabama, Colorado, the District of Columbia, Georgia (if created before January 1, 1997), Idaho (if created before January 1, 1996), Iowa, Kansas, Montana, New Hampshire (for inheritance purposes only), Ohio (if created before October 10, 1991), Oklahoma, Pennsylvania, Rhode Island, South Carolina, Texas, and Utah. The common law marriage will still be valid even if the spouses later move to a different state. There is no such thing as a common law divorce; a formal divorce proceeding is necessary to end a marriage.

Community Property States

In community property states, what you own and can leave by will consists of:

- your own separate property, and
- one-half of the community property you and your spouse own together.

Let's look at both of these forms of property ownership.

Separate Property

In community property states, a spouse's separate property is:

- all property acquired prior to marriage
- all property purchased during marriage with separate property funds
- income earned from previously owned property, if the spouse who earned it keeps it separate—except in Washington, where this type of income is always community property
- gifts or inheritances received during marriage, if directed to only one spouse (wedding gifts are community property)
- property that, despite originally being classified as community property, is converted into separate property by gift or agreement (which must be in writing in some states), and
- property acquired after a legal separation.

Community Property

The system of community property derived from Spanish law, which viewed both partners in a marriage as contributing equally, no matter whose name was on a paycheck, deed, bank account, or other legal document (rather a contemporary view).

In community property states, community property is owned in equal shares by a married couple—that is, each spouse owns 50%. Community property consists of:

- income from work performed by either spouse during marriage
- property and earnings acquired from community income
- gifts made to both spouses
- property that, despite originally being classified as separate property, is deliberately turned into community property by the spouses. This commonly occurs when one spouse makes a gift of separate property to the community, such as transferring the title of a separately owned home into both spouses' names, and
- separate property that is so mixed up with community property ("commingled" in legalese) that one can no longer distinguish the two. In this case, the property all becomes community property. This can easily happen when income from separate property is put in a shared bank account.

Property That Is Difficult to Categorize

Normally, classifying property as community or separate is easy enough, but in some situations, it can be a close call. Here I merely indicate several potential problem areas that may arise. (If you have complications in one of these areas, see Chapter 11.)

- **Businesses.** A family-owned business can create complications, especially if it was owned before marriage by one spouse and expanded during the marriage. The key is to figure out whether an increased value of the business is community or separate property. Of course, if you plan to leave your share of the business to your spouse, or in a way that your spouse approves of, you have no practical problem.
- **Money judgment for personal injuries.** Usually, but not always, personal injury awards won in a lawsuit are the separate property of the spouse receiving them. Indeed, there is no easy way to characterize this type of property.

- **Some pensions.** Pensions gained from community income received by a spouse during a marriage generally are considered to be community property. This community property rule applies to military pensions. However, some federal pensions—such as railroad retirement benefits and Social Security retirement benefits—are not considered community property, because federal law deems them to be the separate property of the employee earning them.
- **Debts.** Generally, either spouse's debts for food, shelter, and other necessities of life are considered to be incurred on behalf of the marriage and must be paid from the couple's community property. Each spouse, however, is individually responsible for paying personal debts. Unfortunately, the line between individual and community debts is often far from clear.

Rules for Leaving Community Property

You can use your will to leave your half of community property and all of your separate property to whomever you want to have it, unless:

- you have arranged to transfer the property by another method (see Chapter 6)
- the property has a separate designation of beneficiaries, as is common for pay-on-death bank accounts, individual retirement plans, and life insurance contracts, or
- the property is restricted from transfer by a contract—for example, a partnership agreement that restricts how you can leave your share.

RESOURCE

Promises made in a prenuptial contract. Agreements you make in a valid premarriage contract are binding and may limit your power to leave all your property as you (later) decide you want to. See *Prenuptial Agreements: How to Write a Fair & Lasting Contract,* by Katherine Stoner & Shae Irving (Nolo).

Common Law Property States

To repeat, common law property states are all states except Alaska (if a married couple agrees in writing), Arizona, California, Idaho, Nevada, New Mexico, Texas, Washington, and Wisconsin.

If you live in a common law property state, the property you own individually consists of:

- all property you purchased with your separate property or separate income, and
- property you own separately in your name, if it has a title slip, deed, or other legal ownership document.

In common law states, the key to ownership for many types of valuable property, whether you are married or not, is whose name is on the title. For example, if you earn or inherit money to buy a house, and title is taken in both your name and your spouse's, you both own the house. If your spouse earns the money, but you take title in your name alone, you own it. If the property has no title document, such as a computer or other electronic equipment, the person whose income or property is used to pay for it owns it. If joint income is used, ownership is shared between spouses.

Separate Property

A spouse's separate property is property held in his or her name. Thus, if both spouses pay for something, but only one spouse's name is on the ownership document, that person is sole owner of the property.

Marital Property

In common law property states, marital property is property that both spouses own together. This consists of:

- property held in both spouses' names, and
- property either or both spouses purchased with income or the proceeds of the sale of property held in both spouses' names.

Rules for Leaving Marital Property

The laws of common law states protect a spouse from being disinherited by the other spouse. The details of such laws vary from state to state, but for our purposes, one general rule applies: You *must* leave your spouse at least 50% of (the value of) all your property.

CAUTION

If you want to leave your spouse less than 50% of your property. If you live in a common law state, and you don't want to leave your spouse at least 50% of your separate property and your share of marital property combined—this book is not for you. Consult a lawyer. (See Chapter 11.)

You are free to give away the balance of your property that is not going to your spouse (if any) however you want to, unless:

- the property has a separate designation of beneficiaries—as is common for pay-on-death bank accounts, retirement plans, and life insurance contracts
- you have arranged to transfer the property by living trust, joint tenancy, or another estate planning method, or
- the property is restricted from transfer by a contract—for example, a partnership agreement that restricts you from giving away your share.

CHAPTER

4

Children

Being a parent may be what motivated you to make your will. Most parents of minor children (under age 18) are understandably concerned about what will happen to their children if disaster strikes and the parents die unexpectedly. In this chapter, I explain how to make specific arrangements in your will for care of your minor children should a tragedy result in no parent being available. This involves two separate, although often related, concerns:

- who will care for your minor children, and
- who will manage money and other property you and others leave them. (How much you leave them is entirely up to you, and I offer no advice on that.)

In your will, you should name an adult, or adults, to handle both functions.

Naming a Personal Guardian

The adult you name to have custody of your children if you and the other parent (if there is one involved) die while your children are minors is called the children's personal guardian. This person is responsible for raising your children. Usually this person also handles any money you've left for your children's benefit, but this is not mandatory.

You nominate your choice for personal guardian in your will. You do not nominate your child's other legal parent, because if only you die, he or she will automatically continue to have custody. You are nominating a person to take over only if neither parent is alive. (Thus, the will forms provide that "if a personal guardian is needed," your choice is nominated.) However, you'll need to name someone else as your first choice for personal guardian in case the other parent isn't willing or able to care for your children. Usually people also nominate an alternate personal guardian, to be sure this role is filled if their first choice can't do the job.

CAUTION

Your choice of personal guardian is not automatically legally binding. Should the need arise, a judge will make the final decision as to who will serve as your children's personal guardian in "the children's best interest." If the other parent is deceased, has disappeared, or has completely abandoned the children, the judge must decide which other adult can best raise them. Fortunately, in uncontested cases (as most are), a court almost always confirms the parent's choice of guardian. But if you think your choice might be contested, you should see a lawyer to do all you can in advance to have your desires prevail if it ever comes to a legal battle.

Choosing a Personal Guardian

For parents with minor children, choosing a personal guardian is obviously a vitally important decision. While many people with minor children immediately know who they want to take care of their children, you may want or need to carefully think about your decision. In either case, when choosing a personal guardian (and alternate personal guardian), remember that you can't "draft" someone to parent your kids. Be sure any person you name is ready, willing, and able to do the job.

The will forms in this book provide space to name only one personal guardian and one alternate personal guardian for all of his or her minor children. Also, you cannot name different personal guardians for different children using these wills, because that requires a more complex will form and perhaps also a written explanation for your decisions.

Each parent should name the same personal guardian(s) and alternate(s). In case of the simultaneous death of the parents, you surely don't want to leave a conflict regarding who will raise your kids.

RESOURCE

More complex personal guardianship situations. Some parents want more choice in appointing personal guardians, and for any of a variety of reasons want to name different personal guardians for different children or explain the reasons for the choices of personal guardian(s). See Chapter 11 for other Nolo resources covering these issues.

If You Don't Want the Other Parent to Have Custody

If your child has another legal parent, that other parent normally has the right to assume sole custody if you die. Legal parents are biological parents and parents who have legally adopted a child through a court proceeding. (Without adoption, stepparents are not legal parents and do not have a right to custody.)

For many parents, it is comforting to know that the other parent will be available to bring up the children. But what if you are strongly opposed to the other parent gaining custody? There's no one-size-fits-all answer here. If the other parent has been involved with the children, she or he will probably gain custody. Judges are very reluctant to take custody away from a biological or adoptive parent, unless that parent is proven in court to be clearly unsuitable for parenting.

A parent's desire to prevent the other parent from gaining custody, however well founded, does not usually determine what happens. Children aren't property, so they can't be left to someone by will (or any other means). However, if it can be proven that the other parent has abandoned the children or has neglected them for some time, a judge may decide against giving that parent custody. The best a custodial parent can do while he or she is still living is to use a will to name someone besides the other legal parent as guardian, then prepare as well as possible for a potential court fight. Preparation can include writing a statement as to exactly why someone other than the noncustodian parent would be the best guardian for the child, and having witnesses capable and willing to testify on this point in court. Dealing with this is beyond the scope of this book, and usually requires a lawyer's help.

Managing Minors' Property

Let's start with a basic legal rule: Minors cannot legally own property (including money) outright, free of adult supervision, beyond a minimal amount—about $2,500 to $5,000, depending on the state. For parents of minor children, this means you need to arrange for an adult to handle valuable property that your children own or inherit. A will is the standard method for making arrangements to handle minors' property.

If you do not provide for this management in your will, and it becomes necessary, a judge will do what you failed to do. An expensive, public, and time-consuming court process for appointment of a property guardian for your children will be necessary. The costs will come out of the children's property, usually money you've left them. The court will supervise, on an ongoing basis, how the court-appointed guardian manages and spends the money.

In writing your will, you'll have the opportunity to address two different categories of property your minor children may receive:

- **Money and other property you leave to your children in your will.** Whether you leave your minor children property directly or you name them as alternate beneficiaries, as many young parents do, you need to arrange for adult management for this property.
- **Property your minor children might receive from other sources after you die.** This may include gifts from other relatives, the child's own earnings, and life insurance proceeds or retirement plans that name your children as

beneficiaries. Some adult will have to take charge of this property legally owned by your children.

The will forms in this book designed for those with children (Forms 1, 3, and 5) address both of these issues, allowing you to:

- set up a children's trust for any property you leave your minor children by will, and
- appoint a property guardian to manage any other property the children receive before they are 18.

Why two methods? A children's trust is preferable to a property guardian for property you leave to your children by will, because it will normally operate free of court supervision. But a children's trust does not cover property your minor children might receive from other sources. By naming a property guardian in your will, you've ensured that you have chosen an adult to manage all property received by your children outside your will, even though this person must be approved and supervised by the court.

Children's Trusts

A children's trust, which is valid in all states, is a legal entity you create as part of your will. The trust merely exists on paper while you live; it only becomes operational upon your death.

A children's trust is included in each of this book's will forms that are designed for use by parents of minor children (Forms 1, 3, and 5). To create a children's trust in your will, all you need do is fill in the correct information, as explained precisely in Chapter 7.

In the trust, you appoint an adult as trustee to manage property you've left to your minor child or children. You also appoint a successor trustee in case your first choice can't serve.

The will forms in this book allow you to create a separate trust for each minor child. You must, however, name only one trustee for all trusts.

Each child's trust ends when that child becomes 35, unless you choose to specify a different age, between 18 and 35, for that trust to end. Age 35 is the absolute cutoff age for each child to receive his or her property, because these trusts are primarily minor's trusts and are not designed for the lifetime management of property. Age 35 seemed like a sensible dividing line between "young adults" and "fully mature adults" (or, youth and middle age).

More Complex Children's Trusts

You need an attorney to draft a trust for minors with complicated needs or problems. The basic children's trusts in this book are not designed for unique situations. For example, an expert lawyer must draft a trust intended to provide for management of trust property beyond age 35 for a person who's bad with money or has other personal habits that may impede sound financial management beyond young adulthood. This kind of trust is called a "spendthrift trust."

The trustee has authority to spend as much of each child's trust income and principal as he or she deems necessary for the child's "health, support, education, and maintenance." This is clearly a major responsibility. The trustee must be sufficiently involved with the child, or children, to know what each needs financially. Thus, the job of a trustee can involve considerable amounts of work, especially if he or she must manage a child's trust property for many years.

Deciding how to allocate money may be difficult. The trustee must decide what is necessary and sensible for the child. Expensive sneakers? ("Everybody wears them.") Expensive...whatever. ("Everybody has one.") Although the task may not be easy, if you pick someone with integrity and common sense, your children's property will probably be in good hands.

Normally, the trustee's main responsibilities—beyond direct concern for the children—are to act honestly and manage each child's trust competently. This usually means investing the trust principal conservatively, keeping good financial records, filing annual trust state and federal income tax returns, and using the trust income (and invading the principal, if necessary) to provide for the children's needs.

The trustee is not normally subject to court supervision. If you have confidence in your trustee, this is fine. There's no reason to waste time and money on court proceedings when a trustee can manage without them.

You may name any adult as trustee or successor trustee of your children's trust. A parent does not inherently have the authority to serve as trustee of the other parent's children's trust. If you want the children's other legal parent to be trustee of property you leave directly to your children, you need to name him or her as the trustee. If you name the other legal parent as initial trustee, it's important to name a successor trustee to serve in case the other parent does not survive you.

If you name someone other than the other legal parent as trustee or successor trustee, should this be the same person you name as the children's personal guardian? Often it's desirable to keep all responsibility for the children unified. But if your choice for personal guardian does not handle money well (however loving he or she is), you might choose to name someone else to manage the property you've left for your children.

The adult you name as trustee should be sensible about managing money. You don't, for example, want someone to gamble in risky stocks, oil futures, or currency. But don't worry about financial expertise. The trustee should simply know the basics of commonsense finance, be savvy enough to put money in a secure money market fund, and be able to balance a checkbook.

Most important is your trust in the person, because your children may be dependent on this person's kindness and judgment as well as his or her financial sense. Choose whoever you feel can do the best job of serving the real needs of your children and, once again, who is willing to do the job.

Your choice for trustee and any successor trustee should be at least 18 years old. If possible, the trustee and successor trustee should live in your state, or geographically close; someone who lives far away may have problems managing a trust from a distance.

Insurance to Benefit Your Children

Many insurance companies will pay proceeds directly to a children's trust created by a will. You simply complete a form on which you name the trust as beneficiary of the policy. However, a minority of life insurance companies are reluctant to allow a trust to be the beneficiary of a policy when the trust will only become functional in the future (when you die). Therefore, check with your insurance company and see what they'll permit. If your insurance company won't allow you to leave the proceeds to a children's trust, you'll have to leave those proceeds directly to your children, to be managed by the property guardian.

Another approach is to create a living trust, which goes into effect immediately, and name the living trust as beneficiary of your insurance policy, with your minor children named as beneficiaries in the living trust for any proceeds from that policy. (See Chapter 6.)

Other Options for Property Management

There are two other important methods that can be used to impose adult management over property you leave to children. Because Nolo designed the wills in this book to be as simple as possible, neither method is available using the wills offered here. The will forms in this book allow only the use of a child's trust, the one method that is available in all states and useful for all children. If you want to use either of the methods described below, you'll need to use another Nolo will-writing resource. (See Chapter 11.)

The Uniform Transfers to Minors Act

The Uniform Transfers to Minors Act (UTMA), adopted by every state except South Carolina and Vermont, can provide residents of all other states with a convenient method for leaving property to a minor child. The UTMA is a model law proposed by a group of legal scholars who make up the Uniform Law Commission.

Both the UTMA and children's trusts are effective, efficient methods for handling property left to minors. With the UTMA, you name a "custodian" to manage property you've left to the minor until he or she reaches a set age, usually 21 (it can range from 18 to 25, depending on state law). The custodian's duties and responsibilities are defined in each state's UTMA. Generally, the custodian can act freely in the best interests of the child. The UTMA can be a very handy method for leaving property to a minor, because it requires very little paperwork. The UTMA is particularly attractive where a gift is likely to be used up by the time the minor is 21—say, for college costs.

The Family Pot Trust

With a family pot trust, you place property left to different children in one trust (thus the term "pot"). The trustee has authority to use all property in the trust as he or she decides is best. With the children's trusts available in this book, one child's trust property, or income from that property, may not be used for the benefit of another child. By contrast, in a family pot trust, the trustee could—for example—spend twice as much money for one child as for another. Thus the appeal of a pot trust: It permits the trustee maximum flexibility to use any property left for the children's benefit as that trustee deems correct.

The possible downside is that one child beneficiary could have little or no trust money spent for his or her benefit, and wind up with nothing when the trust ends, because all trust property was spent for some other family member. A family pot trust lasts until the youngest child reaches the age set for termination of the trust. It often involves difficult tax accounting problems and complex personal decisions for the trustee, who must choose how to distribute the trust property among the children.

Setting Up Trusts for Minors Who Aren't Your Children

You may want to use a children's trust for minors other than your own children. For example, if you are a grandparent and want to leave property to a grandchild, you may wish to use a children's trust and name one parent of that child as trustee. This works well in situations where you have only one son or daughter with children. However, if you have grandchildren from more than one child, the trusts in this book won't work and you'll need a more sophisticated will-drafting resource. (See Chapter 11.)

You also can leave property to someone else's minor children using the trusts from this book, but remember that you may choose only one trustee for all. This means that it's almost always wiser to leave property for other children's benefit outright to the children's parent(s), trusting they'll use it for their children. If you want to do that, you should prepare a letter to accompany your will, stating how you want that parent to use the money for the child. This letter won't be legally binding, but should carry considerable moral/ethical weight. (See Chapter 8.)

The Property Guardian

In your will, you should nominate a property guardian (and an alternate) to manage any property your minor children acquire that isn't managed by some other method (such as a children's trust). Your minor children might receive property from a variety of sources—for example, as a gift from an aunt or uncle, or by earning money from playing in a rock band. If you don't name a property guardian and your minor children receive property of significant value outside of your will, a court will usually have to appoint a guardian to manage the property under court supervision until the children turn 18. This court-appointed guardian could be a judge's crony concerned with maximizing his or her fees, not someone serving your children's best interests.

Here are some rules for choosing your children's property guardian:

- Name only one property guardian and one alternate for all your children.
- If your children have another legal parent and you want that parent to become the property guardian, you should name that person as your first choice, because if a child inherits or receives property, it's not automatic that the surviving legal parent becomes the property guardian. You then name an alternate in case your first choice can't do the job.
- Select someone you trust implicitly, and make sure he or she is willing to do the job.
- If you've created a children's trust in your will, the property guardian is very likely to be the same person you named as trustee of your children's trust. If you trust that person to handle property you leave for your children, there's normally no need to name someone else to manage other property your children may acquire.

The wills in this book provide that no bond is required of the property guardian. A bond provides a financial guarantee that your children's property would be reimbursed should the property guardian mismanage or steal estate property. But a bond costs money, and bond companies are not charitable organizations. Assuming you've appointed someone trustworthy to be property guardian, there's no reason to be fearful about mismanagement, and thus no reason to deplete your estate by the cost of a bond.

Property Guardianships and Children's Trusts

Although it's preferable to have property you leave your minor children managed in a children's trust, it's always advisable to name a property guardian as a backup. Why are trusts preferable to property guardianships? Property guardians typically must make frequent, burdensome reports to a court, which usually requires hiring a lawyer. In addition, state law often imposes restrictions and controls on how a property guardian can spend children's property. By contrast, a trustee of a children's trust is essentially free of court supervision and reporting requirements, and has broad power to use trust money for the child's living expenses, health needs, and education. Finally, a property guardian must turn property over to the minor when he or she becomes a legal adult at age 18, while property left in a children's trust is turned over to the child at the age you specify (up to 35).

Other Concerns About Children

Here I look at some other issues that may arise concerning children.

Simultaneous Death and Minor Children

Parents of minor children are often understandably concerned about what will happen to their children if both parents die simultaneously in an accident. Be assured that your guardianship choice in your will should go into effect if both parents suddenly die, subject to court approval.

By making your will, you are doing your best to make sure that your children have a suitable personal guardian, and that your children's property will be managed by an adult of your choice. Of course, the will of your children's other parent should also be made with these concerns in mind. To minimize confusion in the case of a simultaneous death, the wills of both parents should be consistent with respect to these matters.

Adult Children

The word "children" has two meanings. The first meaning refers to people who are not legal adults, usually under age 18. The second meaning refers to offspring of any age. Under this second meaning, parents can have adult children.

Parents may be reluctant to allow their young adult children to receive significant amounts of property outright, simply because the children aren't mature enough to handle the property sensibly. To leave young adult children (ages 18 to 35) property that will be managed by someone else for a number of years, you can create a children's trust using the will forms in this book.

EXAMPLE:

Carlotta and Ben, both in their late 50s, leave all their property to each other. Each names their two children, Ed and Charles, as equal alternate beneficiaries. Charles is 19 and Ed is 23. Their parents feel neither is yet mature enough to be prudent with money. So Carlotta and Ben each create a children's trust that gives each child his property outright when he reaches age 35. Carlotta and Ben both name Ben's sister, Marcella, as the trustee.

Of course, you don't have to create a children's trust if you're leaving property to adult children, and often it's wiser not to. No one can really predict that a child will be more prudent financially at age 30 or 35 than at 20 or 25. Why possibly restrict the money your child may need—for a house, education, or whatever—for a number of years? Many parents simply feel better to leave the money outright.

Disinheritance

To an outsider, it may seem sad that a parent would want to disinherit a child of any age, excluding that child from receiving any property from the parent's estate. Nevertheless, it's surely been known to happen. It's legal to disinherit a child as long as it is clear that the disinheritance is intentional, rather than accidental.

The wills in this book require you to list all your children. The wills then say that: "If I do not leave property in this will to one or more of my children or grandchildren whom I have identified above, my failure to do so is intentional." Thus, if you do not leave any property to one of your children in your will, you have formally and legally disinherited that child. If you desire to be more explicit and include an express statement of disinheritance of a child as part of your will, you'll need another will resource. (See Chapter 11.)

Normally, you don't have to list any grandchildren in your will. However, if a child dies and leaves children, those grandchildren (of yours) legally stand in the place of the deceased child, so revise your will to list those grandchildren. (See Chapter 10.) If you don't list those grandchildren in your will, they may have a right to inherit some of your property. If you don't leave property to grandchildren listed in your will, the will forms provide, as stated above, that your failure to leave them property was intentional.

If you have a child or adopt any children after your will is done, you should prepare a new will. In the new one, you list your new child's name and leave him or her property (or don't) as you choose. (See Chapter 10.)

CHAPTER

5

Your Executor

Your executor is the person you name in your will to have legal responsibility for handling and distributing your property as your will directs. Your executor's most important job is to carry out the terms of your will by transferring your property to your beneficiaries. Under the wills in this book, your executor will also decide how your debts, probate fees, and estate taxes will be paid, following guidelines set by state law. (If you want to have your debts, probate fees, and taxes paid in a different way, you will need to use a different will-making source. See Chapter 11.)

Your executor is also the person with legal authority to hire a lawyer for any probate proceedings. The reality of these proceedings is that the executor normally does little but sign papers while wondering why the process is dragging on. Your executor is entitled to a fee for services, usually determined by a judge, which will be paid from your estate. The lawyer's fees, unsurprisingly, get paid from your estate as well.

Your executor's job ends once any probate proceeding is completed, which includes having distributed property as your will directed.

RESOURCE

What an executor does: the full picture. For a thorough explanation of an executor's job and tasks, see *The Executor's Guide: Settling a Loved One's Estate or Trust,* by Mary Randolph (Nolo). The book explains in depth each legal, financial, or practical matter that an executor may have to handle after a death. Every executor should have this book.

Choosing Your Executor

The most important criterion in naming your executor is to choose a responsible adult you trust completely. Many people name an executor who benefits substantially under the will, such as a spouse or adult child. This is fully legal and usually makes sense, because an executor who has a financial stake in how your property is distributed is likely to do a conscientious job. Also, by law an executor is entitled to a fee for services, so why not give this fee to a close family member or friend? Of course, the potential downside is that if some inheritors don't trust or are jealous of the executor, there can be bickering or, even worse, serious conflict between family members. Ask yourself the following question: Who do you think would do the best job and be completely honest and aboveboard? Whether or not other family members agree with your choice, ultimately it's your decision.

Be sure to name someone who's willing to do the job. You should discuss this ahead of time and receive your executor's consent to serve before finalizing your decision. You will want to name someone who is healthy and likely to be around after your death.

You should always select at least one alternate executor to serve if your executor cannot. Use the same criteria when choosing your alternate executor as you did for your first choice.

CAUTION

Naming an out-of-state executor. Generally, you have unfettered freedom to name whomever you choose to be your executor. But some states' laws restrict the right of a nonresident to serve. Most of these laws merely require some additional paperwork such as appointing someone who lives in state to receive important legal documents or perhaps also posting a bond. However, the following states impose more serious restrictions:

- **Alabama:** Nonresident can serve only if already serving as executor of same estate in another state.
- **Florida:** Nonresident may not serve unless legally related to will writer.
- **Iowa:** Nonresident can serve only if a resident is appointed coexecutor, unless court allows the nonresident executor to serve alone.

- **Kentucky:** Nonresident may not serve unless legally related to will writer.
- **Nevada:** Nonresident can serve only if a resident is appointed coexecutor.
- **Ohio:** Nonresident must either be legally related to will writer, or a resident of a state that permits nonresidents to serve.
- **Pennsylvania:** Nonresident can serve only with permission of register of wills. Nonresident executor must file affidavit stating that deceased person has no known debts in Pennsylvania, and that executor will not perform any duties prohibited in the home state.
- **Tennessee:** Nonresident must either be legally related to will writer, or appointed to serve with another person who is a resident.
- **Vermont:** Nonresident can serve only with court approval following the request for such approval by the surviving spouse, adult children, or parents or guardian of minor children.

Many people choose their spouse or domestic partner to be their executor. Others select a best friend or close family relative. If no one readily comes to mind as your executor, you have to work through your possible selections, using common sense to decide who would be the wisest choice. Do remember that human concerns are usually much more important than any technical expertise—an executor has the authority to hire experts if he or she needs them.

If you find there is no one at all you can rely on to be your executor, I urge you to keep trying to come up with someone who can serve. But if you really can't, you'll have to see if a financial institution, such as a bank or trust company, will accept the job. Unfortunately, financial institutions often don't work well as executors for modest to moderate estates. Banks and trust companies can be quite impersonal, as many beneficiaries have ruefully learned. Also, a modest estate is unlikely to be a high priority for a financial institution. Still, some people with modest estates end up with a financial institution as executor, because they just do not know any person they trust to do the job.

Terminology

Some states use the term "personal representative" instead of executor. But "executor" works in all states. If someone dies without a will or makes a will but forgets to name an executor, the person appointed by the court to take this position is called the "administrator."

If You Want to Name Coexecutors

With a will from this book, you can only appoint one person to serve as your executor and another person to serve as alternate executor. Appointing coexecutors requires making decisions beyond the scope of this book, such as:

- Must all coexecutors agree before any action can be taken?
- Must the agreement be in writing?
- Can any one executor act on behalf of the estate? And, if so, under what restrictions?

Nevertheless, there are some situations where the will writer decides it's best—for reasons ranging from practicality to trying to maintain, or promote, family harmony—to name two or more people to serve as coexecutors. If you want to do this, you'll need another resource. (See Chapter 11.)

No Bond Required

A bond is a financial guarantee that your estate would be reimbursed should the executor mismanage or steal estate property. The wills in this book specify that no bond is required of an executor. Here's why: The cost for a bond would come out of your estate, and there is usually no sensible reason to have any of your property eaten up by the fees for a bond. If you appoint a trustee you have complete faith in, there's no good purpose for a bond. But if you must select someone you don't know well, or don't fully trust, you may want a bond posted. If so, do not use a will form from this book. You'll need to see an attorney.

Unless you've stated in your will that your executor shall not be required to post a bond, many courts require one before approving a will. And on rare occasions, a court may require a bond to be posted by an out-of-state executor, no matter what you say in your will. ●

CHAPTER

6

Estate Planning

Estate planning means, for our purposes, arranging for the most efficient and economical transfer methods of your property upon your death. This chapter provides a summary overview of major aspects of estate planning so you can see if there are any areas you want to pursue. Also, you may need to understand some estate planning basics to sensibly prepare your will.

Most readers of this book should have no need for extensive estate planning, which requires time, thought, and often spending some money. If a basic will takes care of your needs, why do more? As discussed earlier, most estate planning is primarily a concern for older people who have accumulated a fair amount of property, or ill people of any age. (If, after reading this chapter, you decide to investigate estate planning in more depth, see Chapter 11.)

What Is Probate?

If you die leaving a valid will, the property you've left by will is distributed following a court process called probate. I summarized the probate procedure in Chapter 1. Here I'll note that some state laws permit a simplified probate process for small estates that is relatively quick and inexpensive. A few states, including Texas and Wisconsin, have adopted streamlined probate laws that lessen lawyer involvement and substantially reduce lawyers' probate fees. But in most states, probate remains a hassle. A typical probate process takes a year or more and runs up substantial lawyer fees, usually thousands of dollars.

The main advantage to probate is that it provides a short time period for a creditor to sue an estate. However, few estates—and certainly, very few moderate estates—face any serious creditor claims, so there isn't much of a benefit, if any, for most people.

Another possibly desirable aspect of probate is that a court supervises distribution of your property, which is sensible only if you don't trust your executor.

Avoiding Probate

The drawbacks of probate often make it sensible to arrange to have your property pass outside of probate, especially if death is likely to occur reasonably soon (such as in the next decade or two). Thus, many older people prepare a thorough probate avoidance plan. By contrast, if you're young, you probably needn't bother to arrange to avoid probate now. After all, probate has no impact until you die. As I've already discussed, most younger people are well served by a basic will and can sensibly postpone dealing with probate avoidance for quite a while.

The most common ways to pass property outside of probate are the following:

- **Revocable living trust.** This is the most popular probate avoidance device. You create this legal entity by preparing and signing a trust document that specifies whom you want to receive your property at your death. A living trust essentially functions the same as a will, except it avoids probate. Technically, you transfer whatever property you want to the trustee(s) of your living trust. This requires you to reregister the title of property in your name as trustee of your trust. But during your lifetime, you retain full control over your trust property. You can change or revoke a revocable living trust for any reason, and you can sell or buy any property from or for the trust. No trust income tax returns are required, and you don't have to maintain separate trust records. When you die, all trust property is transferred to your trust beneficiaries outside of probate.

- **Joint tenancy, tenancy by the entirety, and community property with right of survivorship.** As discussed in Chapter 3, each joint tenant owns equal shares of property, such as a house, securities, or a bank account. In some states, joint tenancy property held by a married couple is called "tenancy by the entirety." When one joint tenant dies, his or her share automatically goes to the surviving joint tenants. If you attempt to use your will to leave your portion of joint tenancy property to someone other than the other joint tenant, you won't be successful. You cannot transfer joint tenancy property by will—with one exception: If both (or all) joint tenants die simultaneously, each joint tenant's share of the property passes under his or her will to the beneficiary of the residuary estate.
- **Life insurance.** Proceeds of a life insurance policy pass directly to the beneficiary or beneficiaries named on the policy. Such proceeds only go through probate if you designate your own estate as the policy beneficiary. (This is very rarely done, and not desirable for people using a basic will.)
- **Pay-on-death bank accounts.** With pay-on-death accounts, you name on the account form a person (or persons) to receive any money remaining in your checking, savings, or bank money market account or certificate of deposit at your death. While you're alive, you can withdraw money from the account or change the beneficiary. The beneficiary has no rights to any of the account funds until your death. These accounts are sometimes called "savings bank," "Totten trust," or "informal trust" accounts.
- **Transfer-on-death securities accounts.** Every state except Texas has adopted the Uniform Transfer-on-Death Security Act, which allows you to name a beneficiary, or beneficiaries, for any securities account (brokerage, stock, and bonds accounts) or individual security where you actually hold the stock/bond certificate. This law works similarly to pay-on-death bank accounts. When you die, the beneficiary(ies) you've named for the securities account receive(s) it directly, outside of probate.
- **Transfer-on-death real estate deeds.** A number of states allow you prepare a real estate deed that names a person, or persons, to receive the property when you die. Real estate transferred this way does not go through probate. These deeds must be prepared, signed, notarized, and recorded just like a regular deed. The deed should expressly state that it does not take effect until your death. Unlike a regular deed, you can revoke a transfer-on-death deed for any reason you want, ranging from deciding to sell the property to wanting to name a new beneficiary for it. The states that currently authorize transfer-on-death deeds are Arizona, Arkansas, Colorado, Kansas, Missouri, Montana, Nevada, New Mexico, Ohio, and Wisconsin.
- **Transfer-on-death vehicle registration.** Only a few states currently allow this sensible form of car/truck registration: California, Connecticut, Kansas, Missouri, and Ohio. In these states, if the registration shows a transfer-on-death beneficiary, the vehicle does not need to go through probate.
- **IRAs, profit-sharing, and other retirement plans.** Many retirement plans—including IRAs, profit-sharing, and 401(k) plans—allow you to name an adult beneficiary or beneficiaries to receive any funds remaining in the plan when you die. You can also arrange to leave these types of property to minors with an adult manager.
- **Gifts made during your lifetime.** Any property you give away while you are alive is not part of your estate when you die, so it is not subject to probate. Making a gift during life requires that you completely relinquish all ownership and control over the property to someone else.

Federal Estate Taxes

For all years other than 2010, federal estate taxes are assessed on net estates worth more than a specific amount in the year of death. As mentioned in Chapter 1, the personal estate tax exemption allows a set dollar amount of property to pass tax free, as shown by the chart below.

The exemption is $2 million for 2008. It rises to $3.5 million in 2009. Then, the estate tax is scheduled to be totally repealed in 2010—but only for that year. In 2011, the estate tax will return with an exemption reduced to $1 million, unless Congress takes action to extend the repeal.

The estate tax law is now so complicated and varied that it seems likely that it will be revisited by Congress before 2010. Many estate planners believe that Congress will settle on a permanent exemption amount of $2 to $4 million. To learn the latest developments (if any) on the federal estate tax exemption law, check Nolo's website at www.nolo.com.

For now, if you have a large estate, the best you can do is devise a flexible plan that takes into account the current variation of the estate tax personal exemption. Then, when Congress revises the estate tax law, you may need to revise your plan.

Reminder: I use the term "estate tax threshold" to mean the amounts of the personal exemption in any and all years.

In addition to the personal exemption, all property one spouse leaves to the other is exempt from federal estate tax, no matter how much that property is worth. (However, this exemption does not apply if the surviving spouse is not a U.S. citizen.)

A majority of states have abolished estate taxes, but a few still have them. States generally call them "inheritance taxes." For our purposes, the technical differences between these two forms of state taxes don't matter. Whatever the label, a state inheritance tax means another bite from the estate. But even if you live in a state that has inheritance taxes, they are rarely worth bothering about or planning to avoid, because the tax bite isn't that large (though it can sting).

If your estate, your spouse's estate, or the combined value of your estates exceeds the federal estate tax threshold, you may want to explore planning to reduce your federal estate tax exposure. Why would a couple with a combined estate of, say, $3 million need to worry about estate tax? Assuming the couple owns their property equally, each one's share is $1.5 million, which is under the estate tax threshold for 2008 and thereafter until 2011. So why worry? Because often spouses want to leave the bulk, or all, of their property to each other. When one spouse dies and the combined total of property exceeds the estate tax threshold, it will be subject to a hefty estate tax when the surviving spouse dies. Estate tax planners call this trap "the second tax."

EXAMPLE:

Maurice and Patricia have a combined estate of $3 million. Each leaves his or her estate of $1.5 million to the other. Maurice dies in

Year	Estate Tax Exemption	Highest Estate Tax Rate
2008	$2 million	45%
2009	$3.5 million	45%
2010	Estate tax repealed	–
2011	$1 million	55%

2008. No federal estate taxes are due on his death, because his estate is worth less than the personal exemption for that year. Patricia's estate is now $3 million. She dies in 2011, leaving her property equally to their two children. $1 million is exempt from tax. $2 million is subject to federal tax. With good estate planning, most of this second tax could have been avoided without compromising Maurice's wish to leave the bulk of his estate to Patricia.

The main methods for achieving tax savings here are special estate tax-savings trusts and giving some of the property away while the original owner is alive.

A widely used trust for couples with a combined estate over the estate tax threshold is called an "AB" or "marital life estate" trust. In these trusts, each spouse leaves property in trust for the other (surviving) spouse for that spouse's lifetime. After the surviving spouse dies, the trust property goes to whomever the first spouse named as final beneficiaries. The benefit of such a trust is that each spouse's property is kept separate for estate tax purposes, so the "second tax" is avoided.

One drawback to an AB trust is that the deceased spouse's property is restricted by the terms of the trust and the surviving spouse doesn't have free use of that property. If a spouse may outlive the other by many years, the couple may not want property tied up for so long.

Because of the rising estate tax exemption and the general uncertainty about long-term estate tax rules, a modified version of the standard AB trust has become increasingly popular for those with wealthier estates. It's called a "disclaimer AB trust." Essentially, each spouse leaves all property to the other, but the surviving spouse has the right to disclaim any and all property left by the other spouse. All disclaimed property goes to an AB trust set up by the deceased spouse.

EXAMPLE:

Amanda and Joseph create a disclaimer AB trust for their estate of $3 million. Each has an estate of $1.5 million. Joseph dies in 2008, when the estate tax exemption is $2 million, so his estate does not owe tax. But if all his property goes to Amanda, she will have an estate of $3 million, which could be subject to estate tax when she dies. So Amanda disclaims $1 million of Joseph's property, which goes to Joseph's AB trust. The result is that Amanda has an estate of $2 million, which is beneath the estate tax threshold (at least until 2011). Joseph's trust, worth $1 million, is likewise not federally taxable.

The advantage of a disclaimer AB trust is that it allows the surviving spouse to decide how best to distribute the deceased spouse's estate. An AB trust is created only if it results in overall estate tax savings. When there would be no tax savings, the surviving spouse does not need to establish or maintain an AB trust.

SEE AN EXPERT

Disclaimer AB trusts can get complicated fast. This discussion only briefly highlights the purpose of a disclaimer AB trust. If you think you might want one, see a Nolo living trust drafting resource or a lawyer.

For resources you can use to learn more about AB trusts—including disclaimer trusts—see Chapter 11.

State Taxes

The following states have long imposed inheritance taxes: Indiana, Iowa, Kentucky, Maryland, Nebraska, New Jersey, Ohio, Oklahoma, Pennsylvania, and Tennessee.

However, because of changes in federal and state tax laws, there's a relatively new type of state estate tax that can be a concern for prosperous people.

Before 2002, most states collected a "pickup" estate tax only from estates large enough to have to pay federal estate taxes. A pickup tax didn't increase the overall tax amount paid by the estate. Rather, federal law granted the state a certain percentage of the federal tax due.

Congress changed this system and eliminated state "pickup" tax payments from federal estate taxes. To make up for this loss of revenue, many states have enacted a new type of estate tax—one that is not connected to the federal system. Essentially, this new tax is a "pickup tax replacement." Other states are likely to adopt similar laws soon. The details of these new laws vary from state to state. The common denominator is that estates may have to pay state estate tax even if they are not large enough to pay federal estate tax.

SEE AN EXPERT

If you're worried about state taxes. In most cases, the state tax amount will not be huge. But if you are relatively prosperous and you are concerned about state taxes, see a lawyer in your state who can bring you up to date on this rapidly changing area of the law.

Second Marriages

Members of couples in second or subsequent marriages who have children from a prior marriage often face a conflict about how to provide for their current spouse and also ensure that the bulk of their property remains intact for their children to inherit. A common solution is to use a life estate trust, sometimes called a "property control" trust, which divides use and control of trust property as the trust creator wants. These trusts need to be prepared by a lawyer.

Of course, in some subsequent marriages, couples agree on how their property should be distributed without bothering with a trust. For instance, both spouses may agree that 70% of either's property goes outright to the surviving spouse, with the remaining 30% going to the deceased spouse's child or children. In this situation, a trust won't be needed.

Although a trust isn't mandatory for estate planning in second or subsequent marriages, you should make sure that both spouses, and preferably all children involved, understand and accept (whether enthusiastically or not) how the spouses' property will be distributed at death. If you think there's any realistic possibility of a conflict between any of the players, you really do need a lawyer.

Other Property Control Matters

There are other situations when people want to impose controls on their property and those who are to receive it. The usual solution is to create a trust imposing limits on how and when property may be used. For example, this may be the best way to provide for someone with a physical or mental disability. This is called a "special needs" trust. You'll need help from a lawyer to prepare such a trust.

Incapacity

Part of estate planning includes arranging for who will handle your medical and financial affairs if you become incapacitated and are unable to do so. This is a grim concern, but at least there are simple, binding documents you can prepare to specify a person authorized to make decisions for you, or enforce decisions you've made. (If you want more information on any of these documents, see Chapter 11.)

Health Care Directives

By using health care directives, you can:

- appoint an adult to have legal authority to make health care decisions for you if you can't, and

- provide specific binding instructions for what must be done, or not done, in certain medical situations. A common concern is the use of life support systems. Many people specify for no artificial means to be used to extend their lives, and that they be allowed to die a natural death.

These documents go by various names, such as "advance health care directive," "declaration regarding health care," or "directive to physicians." The document you use to appoint someone to make health care decisions for you is frequently called a "durable power of attorney for health care." Also, in some states, you can use a document called a "living will" (or similar wording) to set out your wishes for medical care. A living will has nothing to do with a regular will, where you leave property. A living will is used only for health care matters.

Many states provide free health care directive forms. Or you can make your own using self-help software such as *Quicken WillMaker Plus* (Nolo). See Chapter 11.

Durable Power of Attorney for Finances

A durable power of attorney for finances allows you to name someone with authority to handle your money matters if you cannot. You can limit this person's authority as you see fit. For example, you can prohibit him or her from selling your home within the restrictions you provide. The person you choose can legally handle all of your financial affairs without any need for messy, costly court proceedings. See Chapter 11 for more information on making a durable power of attorney for finances. ●

CHAPTER

7

Preparing the Draft of Your Will

This chapter explains how to prepare a draft of your will from one of the five forms in Appendix B. You'll fill in written information on the blank lines on a will form and cross out material that doesn't apply to your situation. When you've finished your draft, you'll need to prepare a final version of your will using either a typewriter or a computer.

Let's start with some encouraging words. For most people, the actual process of preparing a will is not very difficult. Pay attention to the instructions, try not to feel intimidated, and go as slowly and carefully as is comfortable for you. Although preparing a will is a fairly straightforward process, it is also an important one that you will want to do right.

Determine Your Family Situation

The instructions in this chapter are designed to take you efficiently through the draft will-writing process. There are different sets of instructions for different family situations. Which set of instructions should you use? Here's how to select the instructions and will forms that are right for you:

- **If you are a parent.** If you are a parent, whether your children are minors or adults, follow the directions for people with children, below. This includes adoptive parents who've legally adopted their children, but does not apply to stepparents.
- **If you don't have children but want to leave property of significant value to minors or young adults.** If you wish to leave money or property of significant value to other people's minor or young adult children, such as your nieces, nephews, or stepchildren, follow the directions for people with children, below.
- **If you don't have children.** If you don't have children and don't plan to leave anything of significant value to any minor or young adult children, follow the directions for people without children, below.

Reminder: If you are getting divorced but haven't obtained your final decree or order of divorce, you are still legally married for will-writing purposes. Be sure to write a new will once the divorce is final.

If you are unsure whether or not you are married, see "Your Marital Status and Your Will" in Chapter 3.

How to Proceed If You Have Children (or Plan to Leave Property to Young People)

From the five different will forms in Appendix B, select the form that best describes your situation, as set out below:

- **A married person who wants his or her spouse to receive most property.** If you want to leave all or most of your property (except perhaps for a few specific gifts) to your spouse—or to your children if your spouse predeceases you—use Form 1. Instructions for Form 1 are below.
- **A married person who wants to divide up property.** If you want to identify and distribute your property among several persons, including your spouse and children, use Form 5. But remember, you still must leave at least 50% of your property to your spouse, or you must see a lawyer. Instructions for Form 5 are in this chapter.
- **A member of an unmarried couple.** If you're a member of an unmarried couple with a child or children, and you want a specific will clause to identify your mate, use Form 5. (This type of clause has no specific legal effect. It is a public acknowledgment of your relationship.)

Otherwise, if you don't want a public statement about your relationship, use Form 3. Instructions for both forms are in this chapter.

- **An aunt, uncle, stepparent, or other person who wants to leave property of significant value to minors.** Use Form 5, which allows you to set up a children's trust to manage property left to children who are under 35 when they inherit. Instructions for Form 5 are in this chapter.
- **A single, divorced or widowed parent.** Use Form 3. Instructions are in this chapter.

Each will form, in Appendix B and on the CD-ROM, is identified at the top of its first page by its number and a description, such as "Form 1. Married With Child(ren), Property to Spouse." To warn you about the obvious, if you tear out your will form, be sure you remove all pages of the form, and no pages from another will form. Each subsequent page of the will form is identified at the bottom of the page as "Form 1," "Form 3," and so on.

If you need additional copies of the forms (for instance, you and your spouse are both preparing wills or you just want extra copies of the form), photocopy your blank will form before filling in the draft. Or print multiple blank drafts from the CD-ROM.

How to Proceed If You're Not a Parent and Aren't Leaving Property of Significant Value to Young People

You'll find five different will forms in Appendix B. Start by selecting the form that best describes your situation, as set out below:

- **A married person.** Use Form 2. Instructions are in this chapter.
- **A member of an unmarried couple.** If you want a specific will clause to identify your mate, use Form 4. (This type of clause has no specific legal effect. It is a public acknowledgment of your relationship.) Instructions for Form 4 are in this chapter.
- **A single, divorced, or widowed person.** Use Form 4. Instructions are in this chapter.

Each will in Appendix B is identified at the top of its first page by its number and a description, such as "Form 2. Married With No Child(ren)." To warn you about the obvious, if you tear out your will form, be sure you remove all pages of the form, and no pages from another will form. Each subsequent page of the will form is identified at the bottom of the page as "Form 2," "Form 4," and so on.

If you need additional copies of the forms (for instance, you and your spouse are both preparing wills or you just want extra copies of the form), photocopy your blank will form before filling in the draft. Or print multiple blank drafts from the CD-ROM.

Instructions for a Married Person—Form 1

Form 1 is designed exclusively for a married person who wants to leave all of his or her property to a spouse, with the possible exception of a few minor gifts. His or her children are named as alternate beneficiaries, who will receive the will writer's property if the spouse dies before the will writer. In other words, this will is "hard wired" to make it as easy as possible to prepare a will.

CAUTION

Don't change the boilerplate language in your will. Making any changes to a basic will form other than simple commonsense changes, such as adjusting pronouns, is risky. The purpose of a basic will is to provide clarity and simplicity. By making changes to the boilerplate language, you risk creating a confusing or ineffective document. If you want to make substantial changes to a will form, you need a more comprehensive will-drafting resource than this book can provide. (See Chapter 11 for a list of other Nolo will-writing resources.)

The Top of the Will Form

Fill in your name in the first two blank lines at the top of the form. Use the name you customarily use when you sign legal documents and other important papers. If you've used different names—for instance, you changed your name to Jerry Adams, but still own some property in the name of Jerry Adananossos—identify yourself with both names: "Jerry Adams, aka Jerry Adananossos." ("Aka" stands for "also known as.")

In the next blank lines, fill in the county or township, followed by the state in which you live.

Will Section 1. *Revocation*

This standard language appears in all well-prepared wills. It revokes (invalidates) all previous wills, thus preventing possible confusion or litigation over the validity of any prior wills. A revocation clause is included in your will whether or not you actually have made an earlier will. You don't need to add or delete anything here.

CAUTION

Destroy old wills. Tear up or otherwise destroy the original and all copies of wills you made earlier. It is wisest not to rely solely on this revocation clause to make them invalid. The revocation clause is legal and enforceable, but someone with an earlier will might be inclined to challenge your current will. Certainly, there's nothing to be gained by leaving prior wills around.

Will Section 2. *Marital Status*

Form 1 states that you are married. In the blank line, fill in your spouse's name. Use the name he or she uses on official documents, such as a driver's license, tax returns, or bank accounts.

What Happens If Spouses Die Simultaneously?

I mention simultaneous death again here because so many married couples are troubled by the possibility of it. As explained in Chapter 2, the 45-day survivorship clause in the will controls what happens if a couple who left property to each other dies at or near the same time. Property left to the other spouse passes to the named alternate beneficiaries. The will form does not have a clause that explicitly addresses the simultaneous death of the will writer and spouse, because this issue is handled by the survivorship clause.

Will Section 3. *Children*

Will Form 1 states: "I have the following child(ren)." In the blank space, list each child's name and date of birth. Doing so shows that you didn't inadvertently overlook any of your children when making your will, which might otherwise automatically entitle them to a share of your estate. The will form provides that if you don't specifically leave property to a child named in your will, you made this decision intentionally.

List all of your biological and legally adopted children, including any children born while you were not married. Do not list stepchildren unless you have legally adopted them. You cannot use your will to (try to) provide for children who may be born in the future. If you have a child after making your will, you need to revise your will (by preparing either a codicil to your existing will, or a new will).

EXAMPLE:

I have the following children:

Name	*Date of Birth*
Jack Goodman	September 8, 1995
Jennifer Goodman	December 14, 1999

CAUTION

Special rules for some grandchildren. Here's something that rarely applies to people writing basic wills, but if it does, you definitely need to handle it. In many states, if any of your children have died, their children have the same protection against being accidentally overlooked in your will as your own children. So if a child of yours has died and that child had children, list all of that child's children in your will. Write "grandchild" in parentheses following each grandchild's name.

EXAMPLE:

I have the following children:

Name	*Date of Birth*
Beth Smith	July 7, 1983
Starr Smith	August 23, 1990
Melinda Smith	January 24, 1992
Benjamin Smith Myerson (grandchild)	May 7, 2007

The will forms state that if you haven't specifically left property to a grandchild listed in your will, you made that decision intentionally.

Will Section 4. *Specific Gifts*

To remind you, specific gifts are items of property you want to leave to a designated person or persons or to a designated organization. Specific gifts can range from family mementos with no monetary value to a house, cash, car, or other substantial asset.

Will Form 1 is designed solely for a married person who wants to leave all or most of his or her property to the other spouse, naming his or her child or children as alternate beneficiaries. The will achieves this by use of a residuary clause, which states that all property not otherwise given away by the will or other valid methods goes to the will writer's spouse, with the children as alternates.

This will provides two options for leaving gifts. The will writer can either:

- make up to three specific gifts and leave the bulk of his or her property to the spouse, or
- simply leave all of his or her property to the spouse and make no specific gifts.

If you're not making any specific gifts, cross off the entire Section 4, and proceed to the instructions for Section 5. You'll renumber the sections of your will before creating your final copy.

To make one or more specific gifts, identify each specific gift (or combination of gifts) in the first blank lines. In the next blank after the word "to," name the primary beneficiary or beneficiaries. Finally, if you want to name alternates, name the alternate beneficiary(ies) in the last blank. Repeat this process for each separate specific gift you make. If you've already prepared a beneficiary list, here's where you transfer that information to your will draft.

EXAMPLE 1:

I leave ___all my baseball cards___ to ___Theodore Zywansky___ or, if such beneficiary does not survive me, to ___Michael Smith___.

EXAMPLE 2:

I leave ___my timeshare interest in the condominium apartment at 2 Park Avenue, Fort Lauderdale, Florida___ to ___Elliott Russell and Noreen Russell___ or, if such beneficiaries do not survive me, to ___Sheila Marks___.

There are no rules that require property for separate gifts to be listed in any particular form or legal language. You need only identify the property with sufficient clarity to leave no question as to what you intended to give.

Most people using Form 1 should have no problems identifying property they leave as specific gifts. They will leave their big-ticket items to their spouse in the residuary estate. But if you want some assistance on how to describe property left as specific gifts, see the instructions for Will Forms 3 and 5, below.

Will Form 1 contains space for you to make only three specific gifts, because most people using this form won't want to make more than that. If, however, you want to make more, that's certainly okay. Simply remove the page marked "Additional Specific Gifts" from Appendix B and make any additional specific gifts on that form. Attach that page to your draft will form, then insert the additional provisions directly after the other specific gifts in Section 4, when you prepare your final version.

The next portion of Section 4—after all the specific gifts, primary beneficiaries, and alternate beneficiaries are listed—states that shared specific gifts are to be divided equally, unless specified otherwise. If you want to leave shared gifts to be divided unequally, divide ownership up by percentages. (See Chapter 2.) Further, the section states that all shared gifts must be sold and the profits distributed as the will directs, unless all beneficiaries of that gift want to keep it, and agree to do so in writing.

The final paragraph of Section 4 explains that a deceased primary beneficiary's (or alternate beneficiary's) share of a shared gift will be divided equally among surviving beneficiaries (or alternate beneficiaries) of that gift, unless otherwise specified. You don't do anything to this portion of Section 4.

Will Section 5. *Residuary Estate*

As discussed in Chapter 2, your residuary estate consists of all property you don't leave by a specific will gift or that you have not left through other estate planning methods. Your residuary beneficiary receives all property in your residuary estate. With Form 1, all property in the residuary estate must go to your spouse. Your children are named as alternate residuary beneficiaries.

To complete this section, insert your spouse's name in the first blank. Then, in the next blank line, insert your child's or children's name(s) as your alternate beneficiary(ies). If you name more than one child to receive your residuary estate you must also state what share of your residuary estate each child should receive. You have two options. You can leave your residuary estate in equal shares, or you can divide it by percentages.

EXAMPLE (equal shares):

I leave my residuary estate, that is, the rest of my property not otherwise specifically and validly disposed of by this will or in any other manner, including lapsed or failed gifts, to my spouse, Henri Vauban, or, if my spouse does not survive me, to my children, Christine Vauban and Emily Vauban-Jones, in equal shares.

EXAMPLE (percentages):

I leave my residuary estate, that is, the rest of my property not otherwise specifically and validly disposed of by this will or in any other manner, including lapsed or failed gifts, to my spouse, Amanda Johnson, or, if my spouse does not survive me, to my children, as follows: 30% to Derek Johnson, 40% to Holly Johnson and 30% to Brett Johnson.

The next paragraph of Section 5 states that if there are two or more alternate residuary beneficiaries, all surviving alternate residuary beneficiaries evenly divide the portion of a deceased one. There are no other options with this will. If you're worried that none of your beneficiaries or alternate beneficiaries will survive you, you could create a third level of beneficiaries by naming second alternate(s) for each alternate residuary beneficiary. However, doing so may create a will far more complicated than what you need. While it's possible to imagine endless levels of disaster, keep in mind the low probability that such disasters could occur. If you want more complexity or other options for handling alternate residuary beneficiaries, see a lawyer.

Finally, the last portion of this section defines "survive" to mean that any beneficiary must outlive you by 45 days to inherit a gift you left.

Will Section 6. *Executor*

As you know from Chapter 5, your executor is the person you name in your will to have legal responsibility for handling and distributing your property as your will directs.

Fill in the name of your executor in the first blank line. You should also name an alternate executor to serve if your first choice cannot, so fill in your alternate executor's name in the next blank line.

EXAMPLE:

I name __Gail Poquette__ as executor, to serve without bond. If that executor does not qualify, or ceases to serve, I name __Maurice Poquette__ as executor, also to serve without bond.

The final portion of Section 6 lists your executor's powers—the authority you give to your executor to manage your will estate. You don't need to add or change anything here. The will authorizes broad powers that the executor may exercise at his or her discretion in carrying out the terms of your will. There's no reason to try to limit your executor's powers, because limitations could cause hassles when your executor attempts to wind up your estate. Because you've handpicked an executor you trust, there's no sensible reason to restrict that person's authority.

CAUTION

Special executor's clause for Texas residents. Texas residents should not use the standard executor's clause found in the will forms of this book. Instead, they should replace that entire clause (including the list of executor's powers) with the special Texas executor's clause that follows below. Using it should make your Texas executor's court job significantly easier, because it authorizes your executor to act under the Texas Independent Administration of Estates Act. This Act enables an executor to minimize paperwork. (The Act can be used in many states. However, only in Texas have courts shown a tendency to interpret the Act to require both specific language authorizing it in the will, and no other listing of executor's powers.)

TEXAS EXECUTOR'S CLAUSE

I name ________________________ as executor, to serve without bond. If that executor does not qualify, or ceases to serve, I name ________________________ as executor, also to serve without bond.

Except as otherwise required by Texas law, I direct that my Texas personal representative shall take no other action in the county court in relation to the settlement of my estate than the probating and recording of this will, and the return of an inventory, appraisement and list of claims of my estate.

Will Section 7. *Personal Guardian*

SKIP AHEAD

If you have no minor children. Cross off this entire section and Section 8 and move on to Section 9. If you include a child's trust (Section 9), you'll need to renumber that section.

Here you name the person responsible for raising your minor child or children, if you and the other parent cannot.

Insert your choice for personal guardian on the first blank line of this section. Name your alternate personal guardian on the second blank line.

EXAMPLE:

If at my death any of my children are minors and a personal guardian is needed, I name __Steven Bronson__ as the personal guardian, to serve without bond. If this person is unable or unwilling to serve as personal guardian, I name Kathy Bronson-Brown as personal guardian, also to serve without bond.

Will Section 8. *Property Guardian*

Here you name your choices for your minor children's property guardian. Fill in the name of your choice for property guardian on the first blank line of this section. Name your alternate property guardian on the second blank line.

EXAMPLE:

If any of my children are minors and a property guardian is needed, I name Steven Bronson as the property guardian, to serve without bond. If this person is unable or unwilling to serve as property guardian, I name Kathy Bronson-Brown as property guardian, also to serve without bond.

Will Section 9. *Children's Trust*

SKIP AHEAD

If you do not need or want to create a children's trust. Cross out this entire Section 9 and proceed to Chapter 8.

As discussed in Chapter 4, you may decide to use a children's trust for property you leave to your minor or young adult children. In this section, you fill in the blank lines to create a children's trust for each minor or young beneficiary you specify. You don't leave the property in this section. You've already done that when leaving specific gifts or the residuary estate.

It's important to recognize that your minor or young adult children could inherit significant amounts of property if your spouse (or other beneficiary) dies before you. Many will writers do leave significant amounts of property to their children as alternate beneficiaries, and so need to create a children's trust.

Of course, if your children don't stand to receive property of significant value under your will, you don't need to bother to establish a children's trust. What is property of "significant value"? Unfortunately, I can't give that term a set dollar figure; life is too fluid for that. Remember, without a trust, property left to be managed by the property guardian must be turned over to the child when he or she turns 18. One approach is to ask yourself, "If my child blows the inheritance at age 18 or 20, would that bother me?" If you're worried, it's a sign you may want a children's trust to protect the young person's property until he or she becomes a mature adult.

Will Subsection 9A. *Trust Beneficiaries and Age Limits*

To create a children's trust, fill in one minor/young adult beneficiary's name in the first blank line. Proceed down the blank lines below for any other trust beneficiaries, filling in a separate name in each line for as many trust beneficiaries as you want to name.

The will provides that each trust ends and each named beneficiary will receive his or her trust property outright when that trust's beneficiary becomes age 35, unless you have specified something different. If you want to choose a different age for any child to receive property, fill in that age in the blank line across from that child's name under the "Trust Shall End at Age" column. You can decide upon different ages for different children.

EXAMPLE:

Each trust shall end when the following beneficiaries become 35 years of age, except as otherwise specified in this section.

Trust Beneficiary	*Trust Shall End at Age*
Grady Watson	32
Daniel Watson	32
Shannon Watson	30

Will Subsection 9B. *Trustees*

Here you name the trustee of all children's trusts you have created in your will. You can only name one trustee and one successor (alternate) for all the children you've named as beneficiaries of a children's trust.

Insert the name of the trustee you've chosen on the first blank line. Insert the name of the successor trustee on the next blank line.

EXAMPLE:

> I name ___Agnes Milgram___ as trustee, to serve without bond. If this person is unable or unwilling to serve as trustee, I name ___Bobbie Robertson___ as successor trustee, also to serve without bond.

Will Subsection 9C. *Beneficiary Provisions*

This clause gives your trustee considerable flexibility in spending trust money on or for your children. The trustee can spend trust money for the children's living needs and educational and medical expenses. The trustee determines what these needs are and how much to spend on them. The trustee must file separate income tax returns for each trust, but a court does not appoint or supervise the trustee. Do not add to or change this material.

Will Subsections 9D, 9E, and 9F. *Termination of Trust, Powers of Trustee, and Trust Administration Provisions*

The last three subsections of Section 9 set out other terms of the children's trust. You don't add or change anything here. Subsection 9D provides that trust property will pass to the trust beneficiaries when they reach the age you specified, or age 35. If they die before reaching that age, the trust property will pass to their heirs.

Subsections E and F give the trustee broad discretionary powers to manage the trust property. The trustee may hire accountants, lawyers, investment advisers, and other assistants. The trustee may also choose to be paid out of the trust property or income.

Congratulations! You have now completed your draft will. You're ready to proceed to Chapter 8.

Signature Clause

The signature clause comes at the end of your will, after the substantive sections but before the witnesses clause. It does not have a section number. Don't sign or fill in any of these blank lines of your draft will or have it witnessed. This only happens with your final will, which is explained in the next chapter.

Instructions for Parents (or People Leaving Property to Children)—Forms 3 and 5

If you have a child or children, or you're planning to leave property to minors or young adults, you'll use either:

- Form 3, if you are single, divorced, or widowed, or
- Form 5, if you don't want to use Form 1 or 3. For example, you may be a member of an unmarried couple with children, a grandparent who wants to set up a children's trust, or a married person who does not want to leave most or all of his or her property in bulk to the other spouse. (But remember, you still must leave at least 50% of your property to your spouse, or you'll need to see a lawyer.)

Now you'll learn how to fill in a draft of either Form 3 or Form 5.

CAUTION

Don't change the boilerplate language in your will. Making any changes to a basic will form other than simple commonsense changes, such as adjusting pronouns, is risky. The purpose of a basic will is to provide clarity and simplicity. By making changes to the boilerplate language, you risk creating a confusing or even ineffective document. If you want to make substantial changes to a will form, you need a more comprehensive will-drafting resource than this book provides. (See Chapter 11 for a list of other Nolo will-writing resources.)

The Top of the Will Form

Fill in your name in the first two blank lines at the top of the form. Use the name you customarily use when you sign legal documents and other important papers. If you've used different names—for instance, you changed your name to Jerry Adams, but still own some property in the name of Jerry Adananossos—identify yourself with both names: "Jerry Adams, aka Jerry Adananossos." ("Aka" stands for "also known as.")

In the next blank lines, fill in the county or township, followed by the state in which you live.

Will Section 1. *Revocation*

This standard language appears in all well-prepared wills. It revokes (invalidates) all previous wills, thus preventing possible confusion or litigation over the validity of any prior wills. A revocation clause is included in your will whether or not you actually have made an earlier will. You don't need to add or delete anything here.

CAUTION

Destroy old wills. Tear up or otherwise destroy the original and all copies of wills you've made earlier. It is wisest not to rely solely on this revocation clause to make them invalid. The revocation clause is legal and enforceable, but someone with an earlier will might be inclined to challenge your current will. Certainly, there's nothing to be gained by leaving prior wills around.

Will Section 2. *Marital Status*

Here you define your marital status. Whether you need to fill in anything depends on which form you use:

- Form 3 states: "I am not married." You don't need to add anything else here.
- Form 5 contains a blank line after the words "Marital Status." Fill in whatever fits your situation, among the following options:

  "I am single."

  "I am married to ________________."

  "My domestic partner (or whatever term you use) is ________________."

Use the name your spouse or partner uses on official documents, such as a driver's license, tax returns, or bank accounts.

Will Section 3. *Children*

SKIP AHEAD

If you don't have any children or grandchildren. Cross off this entire section and move on to Section 4. You'll need to renumber all subsequent sections.

Will Forms 3 and 5 state: "I have the following child(ren)." In the blank space, list each child's name and date of birth. Doing so shows that you didn't inadvertently overlook any of your children when making your will, which might automatically entitle them to a share of your estate. The will form says that if you don't specifically leave property to a child named in your will, you made this decision intentionally.

List all of your biological and legally adopted children, including any children born while you were not married. Do not list stepchildren unless you have legally adopted them.

CAUTION

Special rules for some grandchildren. Here's something that rarely applies to people writing basic wills, but if it does, you definitely need to handle it. In many states, if any of your children have died, their children have the same protection against being accidentally overlooked in your will as your own children. So if a child of yours has died and that child had children, list all of that child's children in your will. Write "grandchild" in parentheses following each grandchild's name.

EXAMPLE:

I have the following children:

Name	*Date of Birth*
Beth Smith	July 7, 1970
Starr Smith	August 23, 1995
Melinda Smith	January 24, 1997
Benjamin Smith Myerson (grandchild)	May 7, 2006

The will forms state that if you haven't specifically left property to a grandchild listed in your will, you made that decision intentionally.

Will Section 4. *Specific Gifts*

To remind you, specific gifts are items of property you want to leave to a designated person or persons or to a designated organization. (See Chapter 2.) Specific gifts can range from family mementos with no monetary value to a house, cash, car, or other substantial asset.

SKIP AHEAD

Specific gifts are not required. If you want to leave all your property to one or a small group of beneficiaries in equal or unequal shares, then you don't need to worry about this section on specific gifts. Cross out this entire section and skip to Section 5.

Will Forms 3 and 5 contain space for you to make just a few specific gifts. Most people won't want to make more than that. If, however, you want to make more, that's certainly okay. Simply remove the page marked "Additional Specific Gifts" from Appendix B and make any additional specific gifts on that form. Attach that page to your draft will form and insert the additional provisions directly after the other specific gifts in Section 4 when you prepare the final version of your will.

To make one or more specific gifts, identify each specific gift (or combination of gifts) in the first blank lines. In the next blank after the word "to," name the beneficiary or beneficiaries (whoever will be receiving the property) for that gift. Finally, name the alternate beneficiary(ies) in the last blank (assuming you're naming alternates). Repeat this process for each separate specific gift you make. If you've already prepared a beneficiary list, here's where you transfer that information to your will draft.

EXAMPLE 1:

I leave <u>all my baseball cards</u> to <u>Theodore Zywansky</u> or, if such beneficiary does not survive me, to <u>Michael Smith</u>.

EXAMPLE 2:

I leave <u>my timeshare interest in the condominium apartment at 2 Park Avenue, Fort Lauderdale, Florida</u> to <u>Elliott Russell and Noreen Russell</u> or, if such beneficiaries do not survive me, to <u>Sheila Marks</u>.

There are no rules that require your property to be listed in any particular form or legal language. You need only identify the property with sufficient clarity to leave no question as to what you intended to give. Here are some tips that may help:

- **Real estate.** Identify a home or business by its street address: "my condominium at 123 45th Avenue, San Francisco, California" or "my summer home at 84 Memory Lane, Oakville, Missouri." For unimproved (empty) land, use the name by which it is commonly known: "my undeveloped 10-acre lot next to the McHenry

Place on Old Farm Road, Sandusky, Ohio." Whatever the real estate, you don't need to list the legal description from the deed.

Real estate often includes items other than land and buildings. For instance, a farm may be given away with tools and animals, and a vacation home may be given away with household furnishings. If you intend to keep both together as one gift, state that in your specific gift—for example, "my cabin at the end of Fish Creek Road in Wilson, Wyoming, and all household furnishings and possessions in the cabin." If you want to separate household possessions from real estate, state that. For instance, "my condominium at 2324 Bayou Lane, Ft. Lauderdale, Florida, but not the possessions in that condominium." Then you could either leave your household possessions to named beneficiaries as you choose, or let them pass as part of your residuary estate.

- **Financial accounts.** List financial accounts as simply as possible. If you have only one account with a financial institution, you can simply list that institution's name and address. For instance, "my account at First Ames Bank, Ames, Iowa." Of course, you can list the account number too, which may make it easier to locate. If you have more than one account at the same institution, you must be more specific. For example: "savings account #22222 at Independence Bank, Big Mountain, Idaho," "my money market account #2345 at Independence Bank, Big Mountain, Idaho."
- **Personal and household items.** You can separately identify and give away any items and possessions with great emotional or financial value: a photo album, an antique, a car, or a work of art. If you own personal possessions that you don't want to bother itemizing, you can list them in categories: "all my tools," "all my dolls," "all my CDs, tapes, records, sheet music and piano." You can lump all your household possessions together: "all household furnishings and possessions in my house at 55 Drury Lane, Rochester, New York."
- **Shared gifts.** Name each person or organization who will receive a portion of the gift, and then specify how it should be divided. You can leave the gift equally or you can divide ownership up by percentages. If you want the beneficiaries for a specific gift to receive unequal shares, indicate the percentage each beneficiary is to receive in parentheses after each of their names, making sure your numbers add up to 100%. The will form provides that, if you don't specify a percentage, beneficiaries will share the property equally.
- **Multiple gifts to the same beneficiary(ies).** It is fine to give a number of items in one blank, as long as the items are all going to the same primary and alternate beneficiaries: "my Rolex watch, skis, and coin collection" or "my dog, Gustav, my iPod, and all of my Bose audio equipment."

Here are some other guidelines on naming beneficiaries:

- **Naming an individual.** List the full name by which the person is commonly known. This need not be the name that appears on a birth certificate, but it should clearly identify the person. Don't use terms such as "all my children," "my surviving children," "my lawful heirs," or "my issue." If you use broad or vague terms, it may lead to serious interpretation problems when you are not there to explain what you meant.
- **Naming organizations.** If you name a charity or a public or private organization, find out the organization's complete name. Several different organizations may use similar names—and you want to be sure your gift goes to the correct organization.
- **Pets.** As discussed in Chapter 3, you cannot leave money directly to your pets in your will.

However, you can leave your pets and money for their care to the person who has agreed to look after them.

- **Gifts to a couple.** If you want the gift to go to both members of a couple, list both of their names. If you want the gift to be shared equally between them, state that. If you want them to get unequal shares, indicate what percentage each member of the couple is to receive. If you list only one member of a couple, the gift will become that person's separate property.
- **Gifts to minors.** You can make specific gifts to minors as either primary beneficiaries or alternate beneficiaries. If you do either, you will probably want to complete the children's trust provision in Section 9.

After all the specific gifts, beneficiaries, and alternates are listed, Section 4 continues by stating that shared specific gifts are to be divided equally, unless specified otherwise. It further provides that all shared gifts must be sold and the profits distributed as the will directs, unless all beneficiaries of a particular gift want to keep it, and agree to do so in writing.

This section concludes by explaining that a deceased beneficiary's (or alternate beneficiary's) share of a shared gift will be shared equally by surviving beneficiaries (or alternate beneficiaries), unless otherwise specified. You don't do anything to this portion of Section 4.

Will Section 5. *Residuary Estate*

As discussed in Chapter 2, your residuary estate consists of all property you don't leave by a specific gift or that you have not left through other estate planning methods. Your residuary beneficiary receives all property in your residuary estate.

With Will Form 3 or 5, you name whomever you choose to take your residuary estate. Fill in that person's or people's name(s), or an organization, in the first blank lines of this section. You can, of course, name someone here whom you've also named as a primary or alternate beneficiary for a specific gift.

If you name more than one residuary beneficiary, decide whether you intend for them to share the residuary property equally. If so, you need only list their names—such as "Cynthia Kassouf, George Cobb, and Bonita Cobb." Each will get a one-third share. If you want them to take unequal shares, you must specify what percentage each should receive—such as "Cynthia Kassouf (50%), George Cobb (25%), and Bonita Cobb (25%)." Of course, make sure that the percentages add up to 100%.

Next, name your alternate residuary beneficiary (or beneficiaries). Your alternate residuary beneficiaries are the last in line of your beneficiaries. They receive your property if your residuary beneficiaries are deceased when you die. Realistically, this is unlikely to occur without there being time for you to prepare a new will updating your beneficiaries. Still, naming alternate residuary beneficiaries provides one last backup against the state stepping in and directing who gets your property. Fill in the name or names of your alternate residuary beneficiary or beneficiaries in the next blank line.

EXAMPLE:

I leave my residuary estate, that is, the rest of my property not otherwise specifically and validly disposed of by this will or in any other manner, including lapsed or failed gifts, to Lee Compton or, if such residuary beneficiary does not survive me, to Taylor Wright.

The next portion of Section 5 states that any residuary gift made to two or more beneficiaries is shared equally among them unless you provide differently. This portion further states that a shared residuary gift must be sold, unless all the beneficiaries agree not to do so.

The next paragraph of Section 5 states that if there are two or more surviving alternate residuary beneficiaries, they evenly divide the portion of any alternate residuary beneficiary who has died. There are no other options with these wills. You cannot use wills from this book to assign unequal portions of a shared gift to different alternate residuary beneficiaries. In theory, you could attempt to create a third level of possible residuary beneficiaries, by naming second alternate(s) for each alternate residuary beneficiary. Attempting this might create a will far more complicated than what you need. While it's always possible to imagine endless levels of disaster, keep in mind the very low probability that such disasters could occur. If you want more complexities or other options for handling alternate residuary beneficiaries, see a lawyer.

Finally, the last portion of this section defines "survive" to mean that any beneficiary must outlive you by 45 days to inherit a gift you left.

Will Section 6. *Executor*

As you know from Chapter 5, your executor is the person you name in your will to have legal responsibility for handling and distributing your property as your will directs.

Fill in the name of your executor in the first blank line. You should also name an alternate executor to serve if your first choice cannot, so fill in your alternate executor's name in the next blank line.

EXAMPLE:

I name __Gail Poquette__ as executor, to serve without bond. If that executor does not qualify, or ceases to serve, I name __Maurice Poquette__ as executor, also to serve without bond.

The final portion of Section 6 lists your executor's powers—the authority you give to your executor to manage your will estate. You don't need to add or change anything here. The will authorizes broad powers that the executor may exercise at his or her discretion in carrying out the terms of your will.

There's no reason to try to limit your executor's powers, because limitations could cause hassles when your executor attempts to wind up your estate. Because you've handpicked an executor you trust, there's no sensible reason to restrict that person's authority.

CAUTION

Special executor's clause for Texas residents. Texas residents should not use the standard executor's clause found in the will forms of this book. Instead, they should replace that entire clause (including the list of executor's powers) with the special Texas executor's clause that follows below. Using it should make your Texas executor's court job significantly easier, because it authorizes your executor to act under the Texas Independent Administration of Estates Act. This Act enables an executor to minimize paperwork. (The Act can be used in many states. However, only in Texas have courts shown a tendency to interpret the Act to require both specific language authorizing it in the will, and no other listing of executor's powers.)

TEXAS EXECUTOR'S CLAUSE

I name _________________________ as executor, to serve without bond. If that executor does not qualify, or ceases to serve, I name _________________________ as executor, also to serve without bond.

Except as otherwise required by Texas law, I direct that my Texas personal representative shall take no other action in the county court in relation to the settlement of my estate than the probating and recording of this will, and the return of an inventory, appraisement and list of claims of my estate.

Will Section 7. *Personal Guardian*

SKIP AHEAD

If you have no minor children. Cross off this entire section and Section 8 and move on to Section 9. If you include a child's trust (Section 9), you'll need to renumber that section.

Here you name the person responsible for raising your minor child or children, if you and the other parent cannot.

Insert your choice for personal guardian on the first blank line of this section. Name your alternate personal guardian on the second blank line.

EXAMPLE:

> If at my death any of my children are minors and a personal guardian is needed, I name ______Steven Bronson______ as the personal guardian, to serve without bond. If this person is unable or unwilling to serve as personal guardian, I name ____Kathy Bronson-Brown____ as personal guardian, also to serve without bond.

Will Section 8. *Property Guardian*

Here you name your choices for your minor children's property guardian. Fill in the name of your choice for property guardian on the first blank line of this section. Name your alternate property guardian on the second blank line.

EXAMPLE:

> If any of my children are minors and a property guardian is needed, I name ______Steven Bronson______ as the property guardian, to serve without bond. If this person is unable or unwilling to serve as property guardian, I name ______Kathy Bronson-Brown______ as property guardian, also to serve without bond.

Will Section 9. *Children's Trust*

SKIP AHEAD

If you do not need or want to create a children's trust. Cross out this entire Section 9 and proceed to Chapter 8.

As discussed in Chapter 4, you may decide to use a children's trust for property you leave to your minor or young adult children. You may also wish to leave property in trust to young people who aren't your children. In this section, you fill in the blank lines to create a children's trust for each minor or young beneficiary you specify. You don't leave the property in this section. You've already done that in the sections above.

Many will writers do leave significant amounts of property to their children or other young people as primary or alternate beneficiaries, and so need to create a children's trust. Of course, if your children and other young people don't stand to receive anything of significant value under your (or anyone else's) will, you don't need to bother to establish a children's trust. What is property of "significant value"? Unfortunately, I can't give that term a set dollar figure. Life is too fluid for that. One approach is to ask yourself, "If the beneficiary blows the inheritance at age 18 or 20, would that bother me?" If you're worried, you may want a children's trust to protect the young person's property until he or she becomes a mature adult.

Will Subsection 9A. *Trust Beneficiaries and Age Limits*

To create a children's trust, fill in one minor/young adult beneficiary's name in the first blank line. Proceed down the blank lines below for any other trust beneficiaries, filling in a separate name in each line for as many trust beneficiaries as you want to name.

The will provides that each named beneficiary will receive his or her trust property outright when that trust's beneficiary becomes age 35, unless you have specified something different. If you want to choose a different age for any beneficiary to receive property, fill in that age in the blank line across from his or her name under the "Trust Shall End at Age" column. You can decide upon different ages for different beneficiaries.

EXAMPLE:

Each trust shall end when the following beneficiaries become 35 years of age, except as otherwise specified in this section.

Trust Beneficiary	*Trust Shall End at Age*
Grady Watson	32
Daniel Watson	32
Shannon Watson	30

Will Subsection 9B. *Trustees*

Here you name the trustee of all children's trusts you have created in your will. You can only name one trustee and one successor (alternate) for everyone you've named as beneficiaries of a children's trust.

Insert the name of the trustee you've chosen on the first blank line. Insert the name of the successor trustee on the next blank line.

EXAMPLE:

I name ___Agnes Milgram___ as trustee, to serve without bond. If this person is unable or unwilling to serve as trustee, I name ___Bobbie Robertson___ as successor trustee, also to serve without bond.

Will Subsection 9C. *Beneficiary Provisions*

This clause gives your trustee considerable flexibility in spending trust money on or for the trust beneficiaries. The trustee can spend trust money for their living needs and educational and medical expenses. The trustee determines what these needs are and how much to spend on them. The trustee must file separate income tax returns for each trust, but a court does not appoint or supervise the trustee. Do not add to or change this material.

Will Subsections 9D, 9E, and 9F. *Termination of Trust, Powers of Trustee, and Trust Administration Provisions*

The last three subsections of Section 9 set out other terms of the children's trust. You don't add or change anything here. Subsection 9D provides that trust property will pass to the trust beneficiaries when they reach the age you specified, or age 35. If they die before reaching that age, the trust property will pass to their heirs.

Subsections E and F give the trustee broad discretionary powers to manage the trust property. The trustee may hire accountants, lawyers, investment advisers, and other assistants. The trustee may also choose to be paid out of the trust property or income.

Congratulations! You have now completed your draft will. You're ready to proceed to Chapter 8.

Signature Clause

The signature clause comes at the end of your will, after the substantive sections but before the witnesses clause. It does not have a section number. Don't sign or fill in any of these blank lines of your draft will or have it witnessed. This only happens with your final will, which is explained in the next chapter.

Instructions for People Who Don't Have Children —Forms 2 and 4

If you don't have any children (and don't plan to leave significant property to minors), you'll use either:

- Will Form 2, if you're married, or
- Will Form 4, if you're single, divorced, or widowed. Also, if you are a member of an unmarried couple without children, and you

want to formally acknowledge your mate in your will, you can use Form 4 for that purpose.

CAUTION

Are you sure you're (not) married? If you are unsure whether you or not you are married, see "Your Marital Status and Your Will" in Chapter 3.

CAUTION

Don't change the basic will form you use! Making any changes to a basic will form other than simple commonsense ones, such as adjusting pronouns, is risky. The purpose of a basic will is to provide clarity and simplicity. By making changes, you risk creating a confusing or ineffective document. If you want to make substantial changes to a will form, you need a more comprehensive will-drafting resource than this book provides. (See Chapter 11 for a list of other Nolo will-writing resources.)

The Top of the Will Form

Fill in your name in the first two blank lines at the top of the form. Use the name you customarily use when you sign legal documents and other important papers. If you've used different names—for instance, you changed your name to Jerry Adams, but still own some property in the name of Jerry Adananossos—identify yourself with both names: "Jerry Adams, aka Jerry Adananossos." ("Aka" stands for "also known as.")

In the next blank lines, fill in the county or township, followed by the state in which you live.

Will Section 1. *Revocation*

This standard language appears in all well-prepared wills. It revokes (invalidates) all previous wills, thus preventing possible confusion or litigation over the validity of any prior wills. A revocation clause is included in your will whether or not you actually have made an earlier will. You don't need to add or delete anything here.

CAUTION

Destroy old wills. Tear up or otherwise destroy the original and all copies of wills you made earlier. It is wisest not to rely solely on this revocation clause to make them invalid. The revocation clause is legal and enforceable, but someone with an earlier will might be inclined to challenge your current will. Certainly, there's nothing to be gained by leaving prior wills around.

Will Section 2. *Marital Status*

Here you define your marital status. How you do so depends on which form you use.

- Form 2 states: "I am married to ____________________." In the blank line, fill in your spouse's name.
- Form 4 states: "I am not married." You don't have to add anything here. If, however, you are a member of an unmarried couple, you may delete this sentence and replace it with, "My partner (or whatever term you use) is ______________."

Use the name your spouse or partner uses on official documents such as a driver's license, tax returns, or a bank account.

Will Section 3. *Specific Gifts*

To remind you, specific gifts are items of property that you want to leave to a designated person or persons or a designated organization. Specific gifts can range from family mementos with no monetary value to a house, cash, car, or other substantial asset.

SKIP AHEAD

Specific gifts are not required. If you want to leave all your property to one or a small group of beneficiaries in equal or unequal shares, then you don't need to worry about this section on specific gifts. Cross out this entire section and skip to Section 4.

Will Forms 2 and 4 contain space for you to make just a few specific gifts. Most people won't want to make more than that. If, however, you want to make more, that's certainly okay. Simply remove the page marked "Additional Specific Gifts" from Appendix B and make any additional specific gifts on that form. Attach that page to your draft will form and insert the additional provisions directly after the other specific gifts in Will Section 3 when you prepare the final version of your will.

To make one or more specific gifts, identify each specific gift (or combination of gifts) in the first blank lines. In the next blank after the word "to," name the beneficiary or beneficiaries (whoever will be receiving the property) for that gift. Finally, name the alternate beneficiary(ies) in the last blank (assuming you're naming alternates). Repeat this process for each separate specific gift you make. If you've already prepared a beneficiary list, here's where you transfer that information to your will draft.

EXAMPLE 1:

I leave _all my baseball cards_ to _Theodore Zywansky_ or, if such beneficiary does not survive me, to _Michael Smith_.

EXAMPLE 2:

I leave _my timeshare interest in the condominium apartment at 2 Park Avenue, Fort Lauderdale, Florida_ to _Elliott Russell and Noreen Russell_ or, if such beneficiaries do not survive me, to _Sheila Marks_.

There are no rules that require your property be listed in any particular form or legal language. You need only identify the property with sufficient clarity to leave no question as to what you intended to give. Here are some tips that may help:

- **Real estate.** Identify a home or business by its street address: "my condominium at 123 45th Avenue, San Francisco, California" or "my summer home at 84 Memory Lane, Oakville, Missouri." For unimproved (empty) land, use the name by which it is commonly known: "my undeveloped 10-acre lot next to the McHenry Place on Old Farm Road, Sandusky, Ohio." Whatever the real estate, you don't need to list the legal description from the deed.

  Real estate often includes items other than land and buildings. For instance, a farm may be given away with tools and animals, and a vacation home may be given away with household furnishings. If you intend to keep both together as one gift, state that in your specific gift—for example, "my cabin at the end of Fish Creek Road in Wilson, Wyoming, and all household furnishings and possessions in the cabin." If you want to separate household possessions from real estate, state that. For instance, "my condominium at 2324 Bayou Lane, Ft. Lauderdale, Florida, but not the possessions in that condominium." Then you could either leave your household possessions to named beneficiaries as you choose, or let them pass as part of your residuary estate.

- **Financial accounts.** List financial accounts as simply as possible. If you have only one account with a financial institution, you can simply list that institution's name and address. For instance, "my account at First Ames Bank, Ames, Iowa." Of course, you can list the account number too, which may make it easier to locate. If you have more than one account at the same institution, you must be more specific. For example: "savings account #22222 at Independence Bank, Big Mountain, Idaho," or "my money market account #2345 at Independence Bank, Big Mountain, Idaho."

- **Personal and household items.** You can separately identify and give away any items and possessions with great emotional or financial value: a photo album, an antique, a car, or a work of art. If you own personal possessions that you don't want to bother itemizing, you can list them in categories: "all my tools," "all my dolls," "all my CDs, tapes, records, sheet music and piano." You can lump all your household possessions together: "all household furnishings and possessions in my house at 55 Drury Lane, Rochester, New York."

- **Shared gifts.** Name each person or organization who will receive a portion of the gift, and then specify how it should be divided. You can leave the gift equally, or you can divide ownership up by percentages. If you want the beneficiaries for a specific gift to receive unequal shares, indicate the percentage each beneficiary is to receive in parentheses after each of their names, making sure your numbers add up to 100%. The will form provides that, if you don't specify a percentage, beneficiaries will share the property equally.
- **Multiple gifts to the same beneficiary(ies).** It is fine to give a number of items in one blank, as long as the items are all going to the same primary and alternate beneficiaries: "my Rolex watch, skis, and coin collection" or "my dog, Gustav, my iPod, and all of my Bose earphones."

Here are some other guidelines on naming beneficiaries.

- **Naming an individual.** List the full name by which the person is commonly known. This need not be the name that appears on a birth certificate, but it should clearly identify the person. Don't use terms such as "all my children," "my surviving children," "my lawful heirs," or "my issue." If you use broad or vague terms, it may lead to serious interpretation problems when you are not there to explain what you meant.
- **Naming organizations.** If you name a charity or a public or private organization, find out the organization's complete name. Several different organizations may use similar names—and you want to be sure your gift goes to the correct organization.
- **Pets.** As discussed in Chapter 3, you cannot leave money either directly or in a trust for your pets. However, you can leave your pets and money for their care to the person who has agreed to look after them.
- **Gifts to a couple.** If you want the gift to go to both members of a couple, list both of their names. If you want the gift to be shared equally between them, state that. If you want them to get unequal shares, indicate what percentage each member of the couple is to receive. If you list only one member of a couple, the gift will become that person's separate property.
- **Gifts to minors.** These will forms do not have provisions for creating a children's trust. If you want to leave a gift to a minor, you can leave the gift directly to that child, with the property to be managed by a parent or parents, or you can leave the gift to the parent(s) to use for the child. If you want to create a children's trust, you'll need to use Form 5.

After all the specific gifts, beneficiaries, and alternates are listed, Section 3 continues by stating that shared specific gifts are to be divided equally, unless specified otherwise. It further provides that all shared gifts must be sold and the profits distributed as the will directs, unless all beneficiaries of a particular gift want to keep it and agree to do so in writing.

This section concludes by explaining that a deceased beneficiary's (or alternate beneficiary's) share of a shared gift will be shared equally by surviving beneficiaries (or alternate beneficiaries), unless otherwise specified. You don't do anything to this portion of Section 3.

Will Section 4. *Residuary Estate*

As discussed in Chapter 2, your residuary estate consists of all property you don't leave by a specific gift or that you have not left through other estate planning methods. Your residuary beneficiary receives all property in your residuary estate.

With Will Form 2 or 4, you name whomever you choose to take your residuary estate. Fill in that person's or people's name(s), or organization, in the first blank lines of this section. You can, of course, name someone here whom you've also named as a primary or alternate beneficiary for a specific gift.

If you name more than one residuary beneficiary, decide whether you intend for them to share the residuary property equally. If so, you need only list their names—such as "Cynthia Kassouf, George Cobb, and Bonita Cobb." Each will get a one-third share. If you want them to take unequal shares, you must specify what percentage each should receive—such as "Cynthia Kassouf (50%), George Cobb (25%), and Bonita Cobb (25%)." Of course, make sure that the percentages add up to 100%.

Next, name your alternate residuary beneficiary (or beneficiaries). Your alternate residuary beneficiaries are the last in line of your beneficiaries. They receive your property if your residuary beneficiaries are deceased when you die. Realistically, this is unlikely to occur without there being time for you to prepare a new will updating your beneficiaries. Still, naming alternate residuary beneficiaries provides one last backup against the state stepping in and directing who gets your property. Fill in the name or names of your alternate residuary beneficiary in the next blank line.

EXAMPLE:

> I leave my residuary estate, that is, the rest of my property not otherwise specifically and validly disposed of by this will or in any other manner, including lapsed or failed gifts, to <u>Joanna Driscoll</u> or, if such residuary beneficiary does not survive me, to <u>Bela Bergstrom</u>.

The next portion of Section 4 states that any residuary gift made to two or more beneficiaries is shared equally among them unless you provide differently. This portion further states that a shared residuary gift must be sold, unless all the beneficiaries agree not to do so.

The next paragraph of Section 4 states that if there are two or more surviving alternate residuary beneficiaries, they evenly divide the portion of any alternate residuary beneficiary who has died. There are no other options with these wills. You cannot use a will from this book to assign unequal portions of a shared gift to alternate residuary beneficiaries. In theory, you could attempt to create a third level of possible residuary beneficiaries, by naming a second alternate for each alternate residuary beneficiary. Attempting this might create a will far more complicated than what you need. While it's always possible to imagine endless levels of disaster, keep in mind how unlikely it is that such disasters might occur. If you want more complexity or other options for handling alternate residuary beneficiaries, see a lawyer.

Finally, the last portion of this section defines "survive" to mean that any beneficiary must outlive you by 45 days to inherit a gift you left.

Will Section 5. *Executor*

As you know from Chapter 5, your executor is the person you name in your will to have legal responsibility for handling and distributing your property after you die as your will directs.

Fill in the name of your executor in the first blank line. You should also name an alternate executor to serve if your first choice cannot, so fill in your alternate executor's name in the next blank line.

EXAMPLE:

I name Gail Poquette as executor, to serve without bond. If that executor does not qualify, or ceases to serve, I name Maurice Poquette as executor, also to serve without bond.

The final portion of Section 5 lists your executor's powers—the authority you give to your executor to manage your will estate. You don't need to add or change anything here. The will authorizes broad powers that the executor may exercise at his or her discretion in carrying out the terms of your will. There's no reason to try to limit your executor's powers, because limitations could cause hassles when your executor attempts to wind up your estate. Because you've handpicked an executor you trust, there's no sensible reason to restrict that person's authority.

Signature Clause

The signature clause comes at the end of your will, after the substantive sections but before the witnesses clause. It does not have a section number. Don't sign or fill in any of these blank lines of your draft will or have it witnessed. This only happens with your final will, which is explained in the next chapter.

CAUTION

Special executor's clause for Texas residents. Texas residents should not use the standard executor's clause found in the will forms of this book. Instead, they should replace that entire clause (including the list of executor's powers) with the special Texas executor's clause that follows below. Using it should make your Texas executor's court job significantly easier, because it authorizes your executor to act under the Texas Independent Administration of Estates Act. This Act enables an executor to minimize paperwork. (The Act can be used in many states. However, only in Texas have courts shown a tendency to interpret the Act to require both specific language authorizing it in the will, and no other listing of executor's powers.)

TEXAS EXECUTOR'S CLAUSE

I name ______________________ as executor, to serve without bond. If that executor does not qualify, or ceases to serve, I name ______________________ as executor, also to serve without bond.

Except as otherwise required by Texas law, I direct that my Texas personal representative shall take no other action in the county court in relation to the settlement of my estate than the probating and recording of this will, and the return of an inventory, appraisement and list of claims of my estate.

Congratulations! You have now completed your draft will. You're ready to proceed to Chapter 8.

CHAPTER

8

Preparing Your Final Will

Once you've prepared a draft of your will following the instructions in Chapter 7, you're ready to finish the will-creating job and put your will into a legally correct form.

Getting Your Draft Ready

First, to reduce the possibility of making a mistake when transferring information to your final will, clean up your will draft. To do this, make sure that all pages are in the correct order and that you've crossed off any extraneous material. For example:

- **Correct any pronouns or other words in the form to precisely fit your will.** For instance, the alternate beneficiary clause in all the forms reads, "…if such beneficiary(ies) do(es) not survive me…." This should be corrected either to "…if such beneficiary does not…" or "…if such beneficiaries do not…."
- **Renumber sections of your will.** There may be sections in the form you use that you don't need. For example, if you decided not to make any specific gifts, you crossed out that section of your will. But once you've done so, the numbering of all subsequent sections of your will is off. You'll need to renumber all the following sections of your will so that there are no gaps in the numbering.
- **Delete the blank lines.** Be sure you omit any blank lines on your final draft. Whether you're having someone else prepare your will, or you're preparing it yourself, cross out the lines on your draft will so that it is clear that they should not be included. Just draw a pencil line through the printed underlines.
- **Cross out the title.** The large title at the top of your will form, and the will form indications on the bottom of subsequent pages (for example, "Form 4"), should not be included in your final will.
- **Make sure all pages are in order.** If you added any extra "Specific Gifts" pages, make sure the page(s) follow(s) directly after the other printed specific gifts in your will.

When you review the will form, you'll notice that the witness clauses have printed material below the blank lines, specifying that the information written above is the will signer or a witness's name or a witness's address. It's fine to leave this identifying printed material on the form, to be included in your final will. Because witnesses' handwriting may not be picture perfect, having the identifying printed material below a witness's writing can be an aid later on. Certainly, having this printed material does no harm.

Next, make sure that your will does what you want, and that there aren't any mistakes. For most readers, the review process should be simple. If your situation is clear and you've followed the instructions in Chapter 7 carefully, your will is okay. But do be sure to check your draft will over thoroughly before preparing your final will. It's well worth spending a little time to be absolutely sure your will says exactly what you want it to.

Now we'll focus on the requirements necessary to make your will legal. Fortunately, the formalities are easy. All you need to do is:

- make sure your will is neatly typed (using either a typewriter or a computer), and
- sign it in front of two witnesses and have them sign it as well.

Below I examine both of these formalities in detail. If your will doesn't comply with these technical requirements—say it was typed but not witnessed—the will cannot be validated by the probate court, and your property will most likely pass as if no will existed. It's not hard to prepare a will correctly. But it's essential to check and double check to be sure you do.

Type Your Will

The final will you prepare from this book must be typewritten. You can either type your will with a typewriter or you can create a typewritten will using a computer and the will forms on the CD-ROM. You can also have someone else prepare your final will, if you prefer.

Do not use a typewriter or handwriting to fill in the blanks of a will form in this book and try to use that as your final will. There are a number of reasons why doing this would be a bad idea. Most important, you'll have crossed out some material on the form, which would make it unusual and, thus, perhaps suspect to a probate judge. A will is not a place to explore unconventionality.

Type or print your will on regular 8.5"× 11" white bond paper. Paper with a high rag content looks nicer, but cheap paper is just as legal. Do not use erasable typing paper.

If you are having someone else prepare your final will, be sure that person:

- receives a neatly prepared draft so he or she won't make a mistake as a result of being confused
- understands exactly where any insertions are to be made in the will, and
- knows that the blank lines printed on the form, as well as any clauses you've drawn lines through, aren't to be typed or printed in the final will.

Using a Computer and a Word Processor

If you have a computer and are comfortable using it, making your final will with forms on the CD-ROM will be easier than using a typewriter because much of the will has already been made for you. You simply need to follow these steps:

- Install the forms on your computer.
- Find and open the form you need to use.
- Add, change, and delete text on the form, using your draft will as a guide.
- Save your will with a new name. Choose a clear and descriptive name for your document, such as "Will of Robert Smith May 21 2008."
- Print your will.

Carefully read Appendix A, which provides detailed instructions for each of these steps.

CAUTION

Note to Mac users. This CD-ROM and its files should work on Macintosh computers. Please note, however, that Nolo cannot provide technical support for non-Windows users.

Using a Typewriter

If you do not have a computer, or would rather not use one, you can type your final will using a typewriter.

I recommend double spacing, although single spacing is permissible. Spacing should be uniform throughout the will. Use standard side and top margins; I recommend one inch on all sides. Number pages sequentially, preferably at the bottom of each page.

Typing mistakes can be machine-corrected, but there can be no handwritten corrections or cross-outs. If you "X" out or type over a mistake, you may inadvertently invalidate your will. Allowable machine corrections include use of self-correcting typewriters and careful use of correction fluid or tape, and then retyping. However, don't do this extensively. If there are more than a few minor changes, retype your will.

Commonsense note: Your primary mission when you (or anyone else) types your will is to avoid any suspicion that you or anyone else changed your will after you engaged in the formal signing and witnessing. Accordingly, if a mistake is made on a sensitive item, say a beneficiary's name, you should retype the whole page rather than using typewriter correcting fluid or something similar. You don't want to create the possibility that a would-be beneficiary, or the probate judge, will question whether the change was valid.

Signing and Witnessing Your Will

To properly sign your will, you must first select two witnesses. Your witnesses watch you sign your will, and then sign their names below your signature. You must do this correctly. Unless your will is properly witnessed, it won't be valid. Happily, it's easy to do it right. Notarization is not required to make a will legal. You won't use a notary unless you make your will "self-proving," as explained below.

Selecting Qualified Witnesses

After your death, at least one of your witnesses may need to testify in court or swear through an affidavit that the document offered to probate is actually your will and that you were of sound mind when you made it. In most states, you can usually eliminate any need for your witnesses to appear in probate court if you also complete a self-proving affidavit. This requires the use of a notary, as explained below.

Follow these guidelines when selecting your witnesses:

- If practicable, select three witnesses, even though only two are required.
- Choose people who are mentally competent and over age 18.
- Do not select a beneficiary of your will as a witness. This is important: If you leave property to a witness, that person may be disqualified as a witness or even disqualified from inheriting that property.
- Do not select your spouse or any of your children as witnesses.

Signing Your Will in the Presence of Your Witnesses

When you're ready to sign your will, call your witnesses together in one place. They need not read your will, and you need not read it to them. However, they must all be aware that you intend the document to be your will. Explain to them that you want them to witness your will and identify the document before them as your will. There's no requirement that your explanation be laden with legalese. You could simply hold up your will and say, "This is my will, and I want you to witness it."

You must date the will and sign it in the presence of your witnesses. In the blanks provided, fill in the day, month, and year you are signing the will, as well as the county or township and state where you are signing it. Then sign in ink using the same form of your name you used in your will. For example, if you start your will with the name of Elissa T. James, sign your will the same way, not in another form such as "E. T. James" or "Elissa Thelma James."

Once you've signed your will, ask your witnesses to date and sign it in ink with their normal signatures and fill in their addresses in the spaces indicated.

Self-Proving Affidavits

A self-proving affidavit is a simple document attached to your will where a notary public attests to your witnesses' signatures. Basically, the notary public signs and stamps his or her seal to a document attesting that your will was properly signed and witnessed. Self-proving your will doesn't affect its validity—it simply eliminates the requirement that a witness appear in person or file a written affidavit at the probate proceeding after your death.

The advantage of a self-proving affidavit is that you've eliminated the possibility that your witnesses will have to go to court to testify that your will is valid. Because you hope your will won't go into effect for many years or many decades, it might be a little difficult, and sometimes impossible, to find a witness after so much time has elapsed.

The drawback to a self-proving affidavit is that you have to locate and pay a notary. Usually, this isn't hard or expensive. Many banks or real estate offices (title companies) provide notary services. You also have to get your witnesses to appear before the notary—a bit more of a hassle. Or perhaps you can ask if there are folks in the notary office who can be witnesses. Your witnesses don't have to be friends of yours. They can be strangers to whom you show an ID in order to establish your identity. This occurs all the time in wills witnessed in law offices.

Even if you don't use a self-proving affidavit, your witnesses are unlikely to have to make a court appearance. There's now a strong national trend among the states to allow witnesses to a will to declare in an affidavit prepared after a will writer's death that they in fact witnessed the will (as opposed to actually appearing and testifying to this in court). Accordingly, including a self-proving affidavit with your will may not be the only way you can free your witnesses from the necessity of appearing in court. But if none of your witnesses can be located at all, and anyone questions the validity of your will (or, much less likely, a judge insists on a witness statement for an uncontested will), your estate may be in trouble unless you used a self-proving affidavit when you signed your will.

If you choose not to use a self-proving affidavit, you can skip this section.

SKIP AHEAD

States where you cannot use a self-proving affidavit from this book. You cannot use the self-proving affidavits provided in this book if you live in:

- **California.** Residents of California don't need to prepare a self-proving affidavit; the declaration contained in the will form that witnesses sign makes the will self-proving.
- **District of Columbia, Maryland, Ohio, or Vermont.** Self-proving affidavits are not permitted.
- **New Hampshire.** New Hampshire allows self-proving of wills, but requires that special language be included as part of the will document, rather than on a separate form. You'll need to see a lawyer if you want to use the self-proving option.

In states where you can use a self-proving affidavit, here's how to make your will self-proving:

Step 1. Locate a notary. Aside from bank and real estate title companies, you can also find a notary by looking in the yellow pages of the phone book or online. Ask if the notary has a form for making your will self-proving. If so, you'll use that form, as the notary instructs.

Step 2. If the notary does not have a form, use the correct form from the four different affidavit forms provided with the book. Either tear out the correct form from Appendix B, or open and print the correct form from the CD-ROM.

Which Affidavit to Use

Use Form:	If you live in:
Affidavit 1	Alabama, Alaska, Arizona, Arkansas, Colorado, Connecticut, Hawaii, Idaho, Illinois, Indiana, Maine, Michigan, Minnesota, Mississippi, Montana, Nebraska, Nevada, New Mexico, New York, North Dakota, Oregon, South Carolina, South Dakota, Tennessee, Utah, Virginia, Washington, West Virginia, or Wisconsin.
Affidavit 2	Delaware, Florida, Georgia, Iowa, Kansas, Kentucky, Massachusetts, Missouri, New Jersey, North Carolina, Oklahoma, Rhode Island, or Wyoming.
Affidavit 3	Texas
Affidavit 4	Pennsylvania

Step 3. Sign your will and have it witnessed.

Step 4. Either have the notary present at the will signing or go to the notary at a later time. Either way, you and your witnesses must personally appear together before the notary. Bring the correct affidavit form that you either tore out from the book or that you printed from the CD-ROM.

If the Notary Balks

Many notaries are familiar with self-proving affidavits and will notarize your document without difficulty. However, some notaries are hesitant about notarizing this document because they correctly understand that they cannot properly notarize a will. If you encounter this problem, gently educate the notary, pointing out that you are not asking him or her to notarize your will, but rather a self-proving affidavit for the will—a document the notary can notarize.

Step 5. Write your name and your witnesses' names and addresses in the spaces indicated in the affidavit, and give the form to the notary. The notary will have you and your witnesses swear to the truth of the statement in the affidavit. The notary will require some identification from you and your witnesses, such as a driver's license, before signing and dating the affidavit and putting the notary seal on it.

Step 6. Staple the affidavit to your will. If you ever make a new will, you must also make a new self-proving affidavit.

CAUTION

Reminder: The affidavit and will are two separate documents. Both you and your witnesses must sign your will in addition to signing this affidavit.

A Sample Completed Will, Including a Self-Proving Affidavit

Here is a sample completed will (by a will writer who lives in New Jersey and used Form 5) after it has been typed, signed, and witnessed. This will also contains a signed, witnessed, and notarized self-proving affidavit.

WILL OF DAVID WARFMAN

I, David Warfman, a resident of Essex County, State of New Jersey, declare that this is my will.

1. Revocation. I revoke all wills that I have previously made.

2. Marital Status. I am married to Melinda Wood Warfman.

3. Children. I have the following child(ren):

Name	*Date of Birth*
Jeremiah Warfman	June 20, 1995
Jasmine Warfman	January 2, 1998

If I do not leave property to one or more of the children or grandchildren whom I have identified above, my failure to do so is intentional.

4. Specific Gifts. I make the following specific gifts of property:

I leave my woodworking tools to my brother, Sidney Warfman, or, if such beneficiary does not survive me, to his son, Phil Warfman.

I leave $10,000 to James Smith, with great appreciation for his skill in gardening, or, if such beneficiary does not survive me, to Melinda Wood Warfman.

Any specific gift made in this will to two or more beneficiaries shall be shared equally among them, unless unequal shares are specifically indicated. All shared gifts must be sold, and the net proceeds distributed as the will directs, unless all beneficiaries for a particular gift agree in writing, after the will writer's death, that the gift need not be sold.

If I name two or more primary beneficiaries to receive a specific gift of property and any of them do not survive me, all surviving primary beneficiaries shall equally divide the deceased primary beneficiary's share, unless I have specifically provided otherwise. If I name two or more alternate beneficiaries to receive a specific gift of property and any of them do not survive me, all surviving alternate beneficiaries shall equally divide the deceased alternate beneficiary's share.

5. Residuary Estate. I leave my residuary estate, that is, the rest of my property not otherwise specifically and validly disposed of by this will or in any other manner, to: 60% to my wife Melinda Wood Warfman, 20% each to Jeremiah Warfman and Jasmine Warfman or, if any residuary beneficiary does not survive me, to the survivors.

Any residuary gift made in this will to two or more beneficiaries shall be shared equally among them, unless unequal shares are specifically indicated. All shared residuary gifts must be sold, and the net proceeds distributed as the will directs, unless all beneficiaries for a particular gift agree in writing, after the will writer's death, that the gift need not be sold.

If I name two or more alternate residuary beneficiaries to receive property and any of them do not survive me, all surviving alternate residuary beneficiaries shall equally divide the deceased alternate residuary beneficiary's share.

As used in any section of this will, the word "survive" means to outlive the will writer by at least 45 days.

6. Executor. I name Melinda Wood Warfman as executor, to serve without bond. If that executor does not qualify, or ceases to serve, I name Sidney Warfman as executor, also to serve without bond.

I direct that my executor take all actions legally permissible to probate this will, including filing a petition in the appropriate court for the independent administration of my estate.

I grant to my executor the following powers, to be exercised as the executor deems to be in the best interests of my estate:

(1) To retain property, without liability for loss or depreciation resulting from such retention.

(2) To sell, lease or exchange property and to receive or administer the proceeds as a part of my estate.

(3) To vote stock; to convert bonds, notes, stocks or other securities belonging to my estate into other securities; and to exercise all other rights and privileges of a person owning similar property.

(4) To deal with and settle claims in favor of or against my estate.

(5) To continue, maintain, operate or participate in any business which is a part of my estate, and to incorporate, dissolve or otherwise change the form of organization of the business.

(6) To pay all debts and taxes that may be assessed against my estate, as provided under state law.

(7) To do all other acts which in the executor's judgment may be necessary or appropriate for the proper and advantageous management, investment and distribution of my estate.

These powers, authority and discretion are in addition to the powers, authority and discretion vested in an executor by operation of law, and may be exercised as often as deemed necessary, without approval by any court in any jurisdiction.

7. Personal Guardian. If at my death any of my children are minors and a personal guardian is needed, I name Esther Warfman as the personal guardian, to serve without bond. If this person is unable or unwilling to serve as personal guardian, I name Sidney Warfman as personal guardian, also to serve without bond.

8. Property Guardian. If any of my children are minors and a property guardian is needed, I name Melinda Wood Warfman as the property guardian, to serve without bond. If this person is unable or unwilling to serve as property guardian, I name Esther Warfman as property guardian, also to serve without bond.

9. Children's Trust. All property I leave in this will to any of the beneficiaries listed in Section A, below, shall be held for each of them in a separate trust, administered according to the following terms:

A. Trust Beneficiaries and Age Limits

Each trust shall end when the following beneficiaries become 35 years of age, except as otherwise specified in this section.

Trust Beneficiary	*Trust Shall End At Age*
Jeremiah Warfman	32
Jasmine Warfman	32

B. Trustees

I name Melinda Wood Warfman as trustee, to serve without bond. If this person is unable or unwilling to serve as trustee, I name Esther Warfman as successor trustee, also to serve without bond.

C. Beneficiary Provisions

(1) The trustee may distribute for the benefit of each beneficiary as much of the net income or principal of the trust as the trustee deems necessary for the beneficiary's health, support, maintenance and education. In deciding whether to make a distribution for or to a beneficiary, the trustee may take into account the beneficiary's other income, resources and sources of support.

(2) Any trust income that is not distributed to a beneficiary by the trustee shall be accumulated and added to the principal of the trust administered for that beneficiary.

D. Termination of Trust

The trust shall terminate when any of the following occurs:

(1) The beneficiary becomes the age specified in Paragraph A of this trust;

(2) The beneficiary dies before becoming the age specified in Paragraph A of this trust; or

(3) The trust property is used up through distributions allowed under these provisions.

If the trust terminates because the beneficiary reaches the specified age, the remaining principal and accumulated net income of the trust shall pass to the beneficiary. If the trust terminates because the beneficiary dies, the remaining principal and accumulated net income of the trust shall pass to the trust beneficiary's heirs.

E. Powers of Trustee

In addition to other powers granted to the trustee in this will, the trustee shall have:

(1) All the powers generally conferred on trustees by the laws of the state having jurisdiction over this trust;

(2) With respect to property in the trust, the powers conferred by this will on the executor; and

(3) The authority to hire and pay from the trust assets the reasonable fees of investment advisors, accountants, tax advisors, agents, attorneys and other assistants to administer the trust and manage any trust asset and for any litigation affecting the trust.

F. Trust Administration Provisions

(1) This trust shall be administered independent of court supervision to the maximum extent possible under the laws of the state having jurisdiction over this trust.

(2) The interests of trust beneficiaries shall not be transferable by voluntary or involuntary assignment or by operation of law and shall be free from the claims of creditors and from attachment, execution, bankruptcy or other legal process to the fullest extent permissible by law.

(3) Any trustee serving shall be entitled to reasonable compensation out of the trust assets for ordinary and extraordinary services, and for all services in connection with the complete or partial termination of any trust created by this will.

(4) The invalidity of any provision of this trust instrument shall not affect the validity of the remaining provisions.

I subscribe my name to this will this 12th day of September, 2008, at Essex County, State of New Jersey, and declare it is my last will, that I sign it willingly, that I execute it as my free and voluntary act for the purposes expressed and that I am of the age of majority or otherwise legally empowered to make a will and under no constraint or undue influence.

David Warfman
Signature

WITNESSES

On this 12th day of September, 20 08, the testator David Warfman, declared to us, the undersigned, that this instrument was his or her will and requested us to act as witnesses to it. The testator signed this will in our presence, all of us being present at the same time. We now, at the testator's request, in the testator's presence and in the presence of each other, subscribe our names as witnesses and each declare that we are of sound mind and of proper age to witness a will. We further declare that we understand this to be the testator's will, and that to the best of our knowledge the testator is of the age of majority, or is otherwise legally empowered to make a will, and appears to be of sound mind and under no constraint or undue influence.

We declare under penalty of perjury that the foregoing is true and correct, this 12th day of September, 20 08, at Essex County, State of New Jersey.

John Stone
witness's signature

John Stone
typed or printed name

residing at 125 Main Street, Clifton,
street address city | city

Essex, New Jersey.
county | state

Amanda Stone
witness's signature

Amanda Stone
typed or printed name

residing at 125 Main Street, Clifton,
street address city | city

Essex, New Jersey.
county | state

AFFIDAVIT

STATE OF New Jersey

COUNTY OF Essex

I, the undersigned, an officer authorized to administer oaths, certify that David Warfman the testator, and John Stone and Amanda Stone, the witnesses, whose names are signed to the attached or foregoing instrument and whose signatures appear below, having appeared together before me and having been first duly sworn, each then declared to me that:

1) the attached or foregoing instrument is the last will of the testator;
2) the testator willingly and voluntarily declared, signed and executed the will in the presence of the witnesses;
3) the witnesses signed the will upon request by the testator, in the presence and hearing of the testator, and in the presence of each other;
4) to the best knowledge of each witness the testator was, at that time of the signing, of the age of majority (or otherwise legally competent to make a will), of sound mind and under no constraint or undue influence; and
5) each witness was and is competent, and of the proper age to witness a will.

Testator: David Wharfman

Witness: John Stone

Address: 125 Main St., Clifton, New Jersey

Witness: Amanda Stone

Address: 125 Main St., Clifton, New Jersey

Subscribed, sworn and acknowledged before me, Beth O'Neill,

a notary public, by David Wharfman,

the testator, and by John Stone,

and Amanda Stone,

the witnesses, this 12th day of September 2008.

SIGNED: *Beth O'Neill*

[NOTARY SEAL]

Notary Public, State of NJ

OFFICIAL CAPACITY OF OFFICER

Letters of Explanation

Your basic will does not explain why you've made your decisions. If you want to clarify your motives and intentions, the best way is to prepare a separate letter and store it along with your will. You can say anything you want in your letter and cover any issues that are vital to you. But make sure your letter doesn't contain anything that seems to (or does) conflict with any part of your will. And to guard against any possible misunderstanding in this regard, state in your letter that you know the letter is not a binding legal document and is not intended to be a part of your will.

Usually, letters of explanation are motivated by love, the desire to express, in writing, deep and caring feelings the will writer has. Here are some concerns you may want to cover in a letter:

- **Unequal gifts.** If you've left more property to one person than another, you may want to explain why. For instance, parents might leave more money to a child who doesn't earn a lot, or less money to a child who has already received part of his or her inheritance. Or a parent may decide that one child's special health or educational needs warrant leaving that child more property than the other children. Doing this can raise serious family concerns—a child who receives less may conclude that you cared for him or her less. Explaining your reasons for your unequal distribution of property can help soothe wounded feelings.
- **Gifts to adults to use for children.** If you've left money or property to an adult, with the understanding that it's for the benefit of a child, you can clarify how you want the gift used. Although your wishes won't be legally binding, they'll go a long way in establishing that the money was for college, not a car.
- **Desires for your children's upbringing.** If you have named minor children in your will, you've prepared for the possibility that they may be raised by their personal guardian. This person most likely has a good sense of who you and your children are, and how you'd like them raised. Nevertheless, it can't hurt to state in a letter how you would like your children to be brought up.
- **Pets.** You can't use your will to put legal requirements on how your pets will be cared for. However, you can make your wishes known by letter. It makes sense to leave details about how to care for your pet, especially if you've left money to help pay for your pet's upkeep.
- **Funeral arrangements.** You may want to express your wishes about your funeral, memorial service, cremation, burial, or organ donation. Be sure to give a copy of these instructions to another person who is likely to be around when you die. Wills are often not discovered and dealt with until long after decisions about final disposition have been made.

CAUTION

Finally, one warning. Don't write anything libelous, such as words another person could reasonably regard as untrue, insulting, or harmful. A letter (or a will for that matter) is not a place to seek revenge or express anger in a written attack. If someone proves in court that the libel in your will harmed him or her, your estate would be held responsible.

Sample Letter of Explanation

December 16, 2008

To my executor and my children:

This letter expresses my feelings and reasons for certain decisions I made in my will. I know that this letter is not my will, nor do I intend it to be an interpretation of my will. My will, which was signed by me, dated and witnessed on December 10, 2004, is the sole expression of my intentions concerning all my property, and other matters covered in that will.

I am giving the bulk of my property to my son John for one reason: because of his health problems, he needs it more. I love my other children, Ted and Ellen, just as much, and I am extremely proud of the life choices they have made. But I believe the truth is that they can manage fine without a substantial inheritance from me, but John is unlikely to be able to do so.

I request that my executor give a copy of this letter to each person mentioned in this letter, and to anyone else my executor determines should receive a copy.

Sincerely,

Lee Monroe

CHAPTER

Storing and Copying Your Will

Once you have properly signed and witnessed your will, your work is essentially done. You have only a couple of small matters left to deal with. Happily, neither of these tasks entails much time or effort.

Storing Your Will

Make your will easy to locate at your death. You don't want your executor, or your loved ones, to undergo the hassles of having to search for your will when they are already dealing with the grief of losing you. Here are some suggestions:

- Staple the pages of your will together. That will prevent any pages from getting lost or misplaced.
- Place your signed and witnessed will in an envelope on which you have typed or printed the words "Will of (Your Name)."
- If you've prepared a self-proving affidavit, make sure it's stapled to your will. If you've written any letters explaining your decisions and wishes, place them in the envelope with your will.
- It's best to store the envelope in a fireproof metal box, file cabinet, or home safe. A bank's safe deposit box in your name isn't a good place to store your will. Banks usually won't open a safe deposit box for someone other than the owner without a court order.
- Make sure your executor and at least one other person you trust know where to find your will.

Making Copies of Your Will

You may want to make photocopies of your original, signed will. A copy of your will is simply a photocopy of the original document that has been signed and witnessed. These photocopies are not legal duplicate originals, because you and your witnesses have not directly signed these copies. The original will is going to be needed for the probate process.

Many people choose to give a copy of their signed will to their executor, but no one else. They figure the executor will be in a better position to handle the job if she or he knows in advance what's involved. Others go further and choose also to give copies to their main beneficiaries, the principle being the more openness, the better.

There is no requirement that you distribute copies of your will. Your will is your own business. You don't have to reveal its contents to anyone, even your witnesses.

Giving close family members or other loved ones a copy of your will may be a good idea if all relationships are amicable, but, sadly, there are sometimes practical reasons not to do so. If you worry that there could be controversy or conflict if you reveal your will to your beneficiaries, don't do it. Recognize, however, that while this resolves the matter while you are alive, it does not address problems that might arise after your death, when the contents of your will become known. If you think some family members or other (would-be) beneficiaries may be so disturbed that she, he, or they might sue to have your will invalidated, you need to see a lawyer. But if the worst you can reasonably foresee is disgruntlement and hurt feelings—well, it's too bad, but it can't, in itself, have any effect on the validity of your will.

CAUTION

Some people are tempted to make more than one original of their will. This means photocopying the original will before it is signed and witnessed, and then having each document signed and witnessed. While it is legal in most states to prepare and sign duplicate original wills, it is never a good idea. Common sense tells you why: If you later decide to revoke your will or change it by adding a codicil, you'd have to locate and revoke each original. Tracking down all original versions of your will can be quite a burden. Or, worse, you might forget one of the duplicate original wills, and wind up changing or revoking some but not all, thus creating a confusing mess and potentially a legal disaster.

CHAPTER

10

Changing or Revoking Your Will

Once you've prepared your formal will using the *Quick & Legal Will Book,* it's extremely important that you not alter it by inserting handwritten or typed additions or changes. You cannot simply cross out something in your will or write in a change. Doing so very probably invalidates your entire will.

If you decide you want to change or revoke your will, you must do so in a legal manner. The laws of most states require that any additions or changes in a signed and witnessed will, even clerical ones, be done by following the same signing and witnessing requirements as for an original will.

When to Make a New Will

Major life changes usually require revoking the old will and preparing a new one. What kind of changes? Marriage, divorce, or having a new child are the clearest examples. Other more simple changes, say, naming a new alternate beneficiary for a gift, can be made with a codicil instead of a new will. A codicil is a written amendment to the terms of a will. (This is discussed below.)

You can use this book to prepare a new will that reflects your current will-writing wishes. If you saved a copy of your will on your computer, it should be very easy to update and prepare a new one and have it signed and witnessed. Otherwise, you will have to create a new one from scratch. Be sure to destroy all old wills by tearing them up and tossing the pieces out.

Let's look at some signals that you should make a new will.

If Your Marital Status Changes

Suppose that after you've completed your will you get married. Or suppose you've prepared your will, leaving all or part of your property to your spouse, and you get divorced. As I've discussed, in most states a spouse has legal rights to the other spouse's property on death. And under the laws in many states, a divorce automatically cancels a gift to an ex-spouse. The alternate beneficiary named for that gift, or, if there is none, the residuary beneficiary, gets the property. In some states, however, an ex-spouse would still inherit as directed in the will. If you remarry, state legal rules become even more murky.

Rather than try to deal with all of these complexities, follow this simple rule: Make a new will if you marry or divorce, or if you are separated and seriously considering divorce.

If You Have or Adopt Additional Children

Each time a child is born or legally adopted into your family, make a new will. In the new will, you will list all of your children and provide for them according to your wishes. If you do not do this, a child might later challenge your will in court, claiming that he or she was overlooked as an heir and is entitled to a substantial share of your property.

If Your Property Situation Changes Significantly

If the property you leave in your will either expands or shrinks significantly after you've made out your will, you should review your will to make sure it realistically reflects your current situation. If it doesn't, make a new will. This is especially important if there are changes in your ownership of real estate or expensive personal property items. For example, if you specifically leave your 1998 Buick to your son and then trade it in and buy a 2006 Cadillac, your son won't get your wheels unless you update your will. On the other hand, if you leave your son "my car," he'll get whatever car you own at your death, even if it's different from the one you owned when you made your will. And if you own two cars at your death, there'll be confusion as to which car you meant to leave to your son.

Therefore, once you acquire the second car, you'd need to revise your will to reflect that fact. (This could be done by codicil. See below.)

If You Move to a Different State

First, the good news: A will valid in the state where it was made remains valid if you move to a new state. So the fact that you've moved to new state, in itself, doesn't necessitate preparing a new will.

Now, the exception: If you are married and move from a community property state to a common law state (see Chapter 3), and your existing will does not leave half your property to your spouse, make a new will that leaves your spouse at least half of your property. Remember, this is required by law in common law states.

If Any of Your Beneficiaries Die

If a beneficiary you have named to receive a significant amount of property (either as a specific or residuary beneficiary) dies before you, you should make a new will. It is most important to do this if you named only one beneficiary for the gift and did not name an alternate—or if the alternate you named is no longer your first choice to get the property.

If Your Children's Personal Guardian, Property Manager, or Trustee of a Children's Trust Cannot Serve

The people you named to serve as your children's personal guardian, property guardian, or property trustee may move away, become disabled, or turn out to be unsuitable for the job. If so, you'll want to make a new will naming somebody else who can protect your children and their property.

If Your Executor Cannot Serve

The executor of your estate is responsible for making sure your will provisions are carried out. If you decide that the executor you named is no longer suitable, name another. (This can be done either in a new will or by codicil.)

Other Reasons for Preparing a New Will

You should prepare a new will if:

- you change your mind about who you want to receive significant portions of your property, or
- any of your children die before you, leaving children of their own. In some states, these children (your grandchildren) may be entitled to receive your child's share of your estate—unless they receive property under the will or you've specifically disinherited them.

Making Simple Changes in Your Will by Codicil

You can make simple changes to your will with a codicil—the legal name for a written amendment to the terms of a will, made after the original will has been witnessed and signed. Codicils are frequently used for small matters such as changes of individual gifts. In a codicil, the will writer revokes a portion of the will he or she wants to change and then adds a new clause. Or the will writer can simply add a new provision, such as making a new specific personal property gift.

A codicil, being a sort of legal "P.S." to the will, must be executed with all of the formalities of a will that were discussed in Chapter 8. The codicil must be typewritten, then dated and signed by you in front of at least two witnesses. These witnesses don't have to be the same people who witnessed the will, but it's advisable to use your original witnesses if they're available. As with your original witnesses, the witnesses to your codicil must not be named as beneficiaries in your will. If your will is "self-proved" with a notarized affidavit, execute another affidavit for the codicil. Once the codicil is completed, store it with the original will.

A codicil form is provided in Appendix 2 and on the CD-ROM. But let me remind you again: For major revisions, don't use a codicil. Instead, draft a new will and revoke the old one. A will substantially rewritten by codicil may cause real confusion. It may not be clear what the relationship of the codicil to the original will provision means.

Here are some simple changes that can be accomplished by codicil.

EXAMPLE 1:

Juliette changes banks for her sole account. She has identified her previous bank in a specific gift in her will, so she prepares the following codicil.

First: I revoke the provision of Section 3 of my will that provided I leave my bank account at First City Bank, Chicago, Illinois to Patsy Vieren.

Second: I add the following provision to Section 3 of my will: I leave my bank account at the Chicago Merchant's Bank and Trust, Chicago, Illinois to Patsy Vieren.

EXAMPLE 2:

John's (the will writer's) brother, Jim, has died. John now wants to leave the player piano he'd left to Jim to Jim's son, Fred. Here's the codicil John executes.

First: I revoke the provision of Section 4 of my will that provided that I leave my player piano to my brother, Jim Baxter.

Second: I add the following provision to Section 4: I leave my player piano to my nephew, Fred Baxter.

EXAMPLE 3:

Kendall has purchased two valuable stained glass lamps. She wants to leave them to her sister, Babs. There is nothing to delete from her old will, so she crosses out the first (deletion) clause of the codicil form. Then she adds the following codicil to her will.

I add the following provision to Section 3 of my will:
I leave my two stained glass lamps from the 1900s to my sister, Babs Zelinsky or, if she does not survive me, to my niece, Letitia Moore.

Be sure anyone with a copy of your will receives a copy of the codicil. This may be a nuisance, but will prevent confusion, or even conflict, later. The codicil doesn't have to be made part of the signature page of the original will. It must, however, refer to that will. This can be simply accomplished by labeling the codicil document "first codicil of the will of ____[your name]____, dated ____[give date will was originally prepared]____." The entire will is now considered to have been prepared as of the date of the codicil.

Don't prepare more than one codicil. If you need to make further changes in your will, prepare a new will. Having two or more codicils can lead to confusion regarding what's in or out of your will.

Revoking Your Will

Anyone who writes a will should understand how it can be revoked. There are only two ways: first, by deliberate act of the will writer; second, by operation of law. Let's look at each of these.

Deliberate Act to Revoke a Will

A will writer who wants to revoke a prior will should do so by express written statement in his or her new will. All the will forms in this book provide that the will writer revokes any previous wills.

Many states' laws provide that an existing will (or codicil) is also revoked by being "burnt, torn, concealed, defaced, obliterated or destroyed" (or similar wording) if the will writer intended to revoke it with that action. This can be legally accomplished by someone other than the will writer at his or her direction. The problem with destroying a will, or having someone else do so, is that this only serves to revoke the will if you intend it to. After your death, this can become a matter of controversy, especially if you've distributed copies of your original will. So, if you want the satisfaction of destroying a revoked will, go right ahead—but, to be secure, make certain you've also revoked it in writing in your new will.

Revocation of Will Provisions by Act of Law

As is discussed in Chapter 3, a spouse in a common law state has a statutory right to a certain percentage of the other spouse's estate (unless that right has been waived by a written marital agreement). And, as discussed in Chapter 4, children not mentioned in a will have statutory rights to a part of a parent's estate.

So the law revokes the portions of a will that do not provide for a spouse or an unmentioned child, but it leaves all other provisions intact. With a will drafted from this book, you shouldn't have to concern yourself with this. If you followed the instructions, you've suitably provided for your spouse and you've mentioned all your children in your will.

CHAPTER

11

Going Further

Some readers may decide they want to learn more about the options for will writing or explore estate planning concerns beyond what is offered in this book. Here I discuss other Nolo resources that provide information beyond the scope of this book. I also cover some realistic points about hiring a lawyer.

Other Will-Writing Options

Nolo's Simple Will Book, by Denis Clifford (Nolo), *Nolo's Online Will*, and *Quicken WillMaker Plus* (Nolo's will software) offer many options for a will that are not included in this basic book. Each provides broader coverage of possible will issues, and give a more in-depth discussion of essential will matters. Additional issues covered in these resources include:

- **A debt-forgiveness clause.** One type of "gift" you can leave in your will is to forgive debts owed to you. If you don't, the debt remains alive, and the debtor will need to pay it to your estate.
- **A clause providing what estate resources are to be used to pay any last debts and taxes.** If you don't specify, this is normally decided by your executor.
- **A clause naming different personal guardians for different children.** In some situations, a will writer feels different personal guardians would be in the children's best interest.
- **A clause where you can state specific reasons why the personal guardian you've named for your children is the best choice.** This explanation may be persuasive in a variety of circumstances, particularly where a custodial parent objects to the other parent raising the children.
- **A clause where you can name different property guardians for different children.** Again, this is for situations where the will writer decides different property guardians would be in the children's best interest.
- **An express disinheritance clause.** This can be used by people who want to explicitly exclude someone (particularly a child) from receiving any property under the will. (This clause is available only in *Nolo's Simple Will Book.*)
- **A clause covering mortgages on real estate.** If you leave some real estate (for example, a house) and don't mention anything about the mortgage on that property, the mortgage goes with the gift. This clause allows you to give the gift free of the mortgage, which must be paid off from other specified assets in your estate. (Only *Nolo's Simple Will Book* covers this issue.)
- **Options for adult management of property left to minors, other than a children's trust.** Your two other choices are leaving property through either the Uniform Gifts to Minors Act or in a family pot trust (both discussed in Chapter 4).
- **A pet bequest clause.** This is a unique clause designed to leave your pet to someone you trust to care for it when you die. The clause names your pet and allows you to leave money to the caretaker specifically for your pet's care. (This clause is available only in *Quicken WillMaker Plus.*) However, you don't need this specially worded clause to leave your pet to someone—you can do that with any will, including those provided in this book. (See Rule 6 in Chapter 3.)

For General Information on Estate Planning

Plan Your Estate, by Denis Clifford (Nolo), discusses all significant issues of estate planning and provides information relevant to all sizes of estates, from the very modest to the very wealthy. Even if you eventually decide you need to see a lawyer, reading *Plan Your Estate* will help you to become an educated consumer, so that you can evaluate whether you're getting your money's worth.

Probate-Avoiding Living Trusts

I discussed reasons to avoid probate in Chapter 6. If you decide you want to further investigate creating a living trust to avoid probate, Nolo provides you with choices: *Make Your Own Living Trust,* by Denis Clifford (Nolo), *Nolo's Online Living Trust,* and *Quicken WillMaker Plus.* Each provides thorough explanations of what a living trust is and does and allows you to create your own living trust.

Creating an AB Trust for Estate Tax Savings

Make Your Own Living Trust and *Quicken WillMaker Plus* provide the information and forms you need to create an AB trust. This type of trust is for couples with combined net estates over the estate tax threshold. (See Chapter 6.)

Creating Documents for Health Care

Quicken WillMaker Plus (Nolo) allows you to create your documents regarding health care. Commonly, you'll use two: a declaration to physicians and a durable power of attorney for health care. These forms are specifically geared to be valid under your state's laws. They are legally binding documents in which you authorize someone else to make medical decisions for you, or enforce your specific instructions, if you become incompetent and unable to make or enforce your own decisions.

The documents in *Quicken WillMaker Plus* are limited to carrying out your wishes for health care if you are terminally ill and unable to express your wishes at the time, or if you are in a permanent coma. They are not appropriate for other contexts where you might wish to have someone make your health care decisions for you, such as if you develop Alzheimer's disease or become mentally ill.

Creating a Durable Power of Attorney for Finances

You can create a durable power of attorney for finances using *Quicken WillMaker Plus.*

Other Nolo Estate Planning Resources

In addition to the books and software mentioned, Nolo offers other books on various aspects of estate planning, including:

- *The Executor's Guide: Settling a Loved One's Estate or Trust,* by Mary Randolph (Nolo), explains what a will executor actually needs to do. It covers legal, financial, and practical matters that must be resolved after a death.
- *The Busy Family's Guide to Estate Planning: 10 Steps to Peace of Mind,* by Liza Weiman Hanks (Nolo), is a clear guide for new parents to real-world planning concerns. It distinguishes what's wise to do now—such as choosing a guardian for minor children and preparing a will—and what can wait until later.
- *Estate Planning Basics,* by Denis Clifford (Nolo), is a straightforward explanation of the key aspects of estate planning that can matter to regular folks, without wading through options for the very rich.
- *Special Needs Trusts: Protect Your Child's Financial Future,* Stephen R. Elias (Nolo), provides information and forms for creating a trust for a person with a disability that preserves eligibility for government assistance programs.
- *8 Ways to Avoid Probate,* by Mary Randolph (Nolo), details easy-to-use strategies for those who want to avoid probate.
- *Long-Term Care: How to Plan & Pay for It,* by Joseph L. Matthews (Nolo), explains your options and choices for finding the right kind of long-term care in the right place, for a fair price.

Enjoying Retirement

Those "golden years" may actually be gold if you're fortunate. This does not at all mean you must be rich to be able to enjoy retirement. There's a large financial industry in the U.S. devoted to scaring people into believing that retirement is only about making the right investments. For a sane and inspiring view of what retirement really involves, read *Get a Life: You Don't Need a Million to Retire Well,* by Ralph Warner (Nolo). The keys to a fulfilling old(er) age, as Warner discusses in depth, are maintaining good health, relationships, family ties, and varied interests, activities, even passions—and enough money to live in comfort, if not opulence.

Using Lawyers

While this book is designed for do-it-yourself preparation of your own basic will, there will certainly be some readers who discover that they want to see a lawyer. Here I discuss when that is feasible or needed.

Hiring a Lawyer to Review Your Will

Hiring a lawyer solely to review the will you've prepared sounds like a good idea. It shouldn't cost much and seems to offer a comforting security. Sadly, though, it may be difficult or even impossible to find a lawyer who will accept the job.

While this is unfortunate, I'm not willing to excoriate lawyers who won't review a do-it-yourself will. From their point of view, they are being asked to accept what can turn into a significant responsibility for what they regard as inadequate compensation, given their usual fees. Any prudent lawyer sees every client as a potential occasion for a malpractice claim or, at least, serious later hassles—a phone call four years down the line that begins, "We talked to you about our wills, and now…." Many experienced lawyers want to avoid this kind of risk. Also, many lawyers feel that if they're only reviewing someone else's work, they simply don't get deeply enough into a situation to be sure of their opinions. All you can do here is to keep trying to find a sympathetic lawyer—or be prepared to pay enough that the lawyer can feel she or he has been compensated adequately to review your will.

Situations Where You'll Need a Lawyer

There are certainly instances where you will need to hire a lawyer for assistance in will writing and estate planning. Some common situations are where:

- you want a special needs trust for a disadvantaged child or family member
- you think someone will contest your will
- you're in a second or subsequent marriage where at least one spouse has children from a prior marriage, and you have concerns that there may be conflict between your spouse and your children over your property disposition
- your individual estate exceeds the federal estate tax threshold
- you and your spouse's combined estate is over the federal estate tax threshold and you decide you do not want to create an AB trust using *Make Your Own Living Trust,* or *Quicken WillMaker Plus*
- you want to put restrictions on your gifts, such as controlling how long one beneficiary has use of a gift before the property goes to another beneficiary.

This is not an exhaustive list, of course. When human beings, property, love and other emotions, death, and law all intersect, the possibilities for complexities are endless.

If you want a discussion of how to find a lawyer, check any of the Nolo resources listed in this chapter. Here I don't cover in depth how to find a lawyer if you need one. Most readers of this book simply won't need a lawyer. If you do, asking around is the best route. Try to find someone who's used a lawyer for a will or estate plan and is satisfied with what she or he got. Ask friends, work associates, and anyone you know who's in business for themselves—this will often yield at least a referral to a reliable will/estate planning lawyer.

Another approach is to use Nolo's Lawyer Directory which provides detailed profiles of attorney advertisers, including information about the lawyer's education, experience, practice areas, and fee schedule. Go to www.lawyers.nolo.com or Nolo's main website at www.nolo.com.

If you see a lawyer, I urge you—double urge you—not to be intimidated. Be sure you feel at ease with the lawyer, and that he or she is willing to work *with* you (not just tell you he or she has "finished" your work) and gives you a clear estimate of his or her charges for the work.

Let me conclude by reminding you that if your desires are clear and your situation is straightforward, you can, as I've been reiterating throughout this book, safely prepare your will on your own. ●

APPENDIX

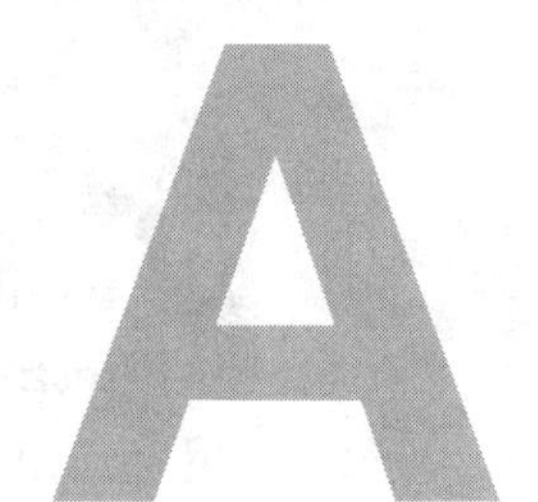

How to Use the CD-ROM

Please read this appendix and the ReadMe.txt file included on the CD-ROM for instructions on using it.

In accordance with U.S. copyright laws, the CD-ROM and its files are for your personal use only.

The CD-ROM can be used with Windows computers. It is not a stand-alone software program. It installs files that use software programs that need to be on your computer already.

Note to Macintosh users: This CD-ROM and its files should work on Macintosh computers. Please note, however, that Nolo cannot provide technical support for non-Windows users.

How to View the ReadMe File

To view the ReadMe.txt file, insert the CD-ROM into your computer's CD-ROM drive and follow these instructions.

- **Windows 2000, XP, and Vista:** (1) On your computer's desktop, double click the My Computer icon; (2) double click the icon for the CD-ROM drive into which the Forms CD-ROM was inserted; (3) double click the ReadMe.txt file.
- **Macintosh:** (1) On your Mac desktop, double click the icon for the CD-ROM that you inserted; (2) double click on the ReadMe.txt file.

Installing the Form Files Onto Your Computer

Before you can do anything with the files on the CD-ROM, you need to install them onto your computer.

Insert the CD-ROM and do the following.

Windows 2000, XP, and Vista

Follow the instructions that appear on the screen.

If nothing happens when you insert the CD-ROM, then (1) double click the My Computer icon; (2) double click the icon for the CD-ROM drive that you inserted the CD-ROM into; (3) double click the file Setup.exe.

Macintosh

If the Will Forms CD window is not open, open it by double clicking the Will Forms CD icon.

(1) Select the Will Forms folder icon and (2) drag the folder icon onto your computer.

Where Are the Files Installed?

Windows 2000, XP, and Vista

- RTF files are installed by default to a folder named \Will Forms in the \Program Files folder of your computer.

Macintosh

- RTF files are located in the Will Forms folder.

Using the Word Processing Files to Create Documents

The CD-ROM includes word processing files that you can open, complete, print, and save with your word processing program. All word processing forms come in rich text format and have the extension .rtf. For example, the Will Codicil discussed in Chapter 10 is on the file Codicil.rtf. RTF files can be read by most recent word processing programs including Microsoft *Word*, Windows *WordPad*, and recent versions of *WordPerfect*.

The following are general instructions. Because each word processor uses different commands to open, format, save, and print documents, refer to your word processor's help file for specific instructions.

Do not call Nolo's technical support if you have questions on how to use your word processor or your computer.

Opening a File

You can open word processing files with any of the three following ways:

1. Windows users can open a file by selecting its shortcut. (1) Click the Windows Start button; (2) open the Programs folder; (3) open the Will Forms folder; (4) click the shortcut to the form you want to work with.
2. Both Windows and Macintosh users can open a file by double clicking it. (1) Use My Computer or Windows Explorer (Windows 2000, XP, or Vista) or the Finder (Macintosh) to go to the Will Forms folder and (2) double click the file you want to open.
3. Windows and Macintosh users can open a file from within their word processing program. (1) Open your word processing program; (2) go to the File menu and choose the Open command. This opens a dialog box where (3) you will select the location and name of the file. (You will navigate to the version of the Will Forms folder that you've installed on your computer.)

Editing Your Document

Here are tips for working on your document.

Refer to the book's instructions and sample agreements for help.

Underlines indicate where to enter information, frequently including bracketed instructions. Delete the underlines and instructions before finishing your document.

Signature lines should appear on a page with at least some text from the document itself.

Printing Out the Document

Use your word processing program's or text editor's Print command to print out your document.

Saving Your Document

Use the Save As command to save and rename your document. You will be unable to use the Save command because the files are read-only. If you save the file without renaming it, the underlines that indicate where you need to enter your information will be lost, and you will be unable to create a new document with this file without recopying the original file from the CD-ROM.

Files on the CD-ROM

The following word processing files are in rich text format (RTF):

Form Name	File Name
Self-Proving Affidavit: Form 1	Affidavit1.rtf
Self-Proving Affidavit: Form 2	Affidavit2.rtf
Self-Proving Affidavit: Texas	Affidavit_TX.rtf
Self-Proving Affidavit: Pennsylvania	Affidavit_PA.rtf
Beneficiary Worksheet	Beneficiary.rtf
Will Codicil	Codicil.rtf
Additional Specific Gifts	SpecificGifts.rtf
Will Form 1. Married With Child(ren), Property to Spouse	WillForm1.rtf
Will Form 2. Married With No Children	WillForm2.rtf
Will Form 3. Single, Divorced or Widowed With Child(ren)	WillForm3.rtf
Will Form 4. Single, Divorced or Widowed With No Children	WillForm4.rtf
Will Form 5. All-Purpose Will	WillForm5.rtf

APPENDIX

B

Forms

Will Forms

Will Form 1. Married With Child(ren), Property to Spouse

Will Form 2. Married With No Children

Will Form 3. Single, Divorced, or Widowed With Child(ren)

Will Form 4. Single, Divorced, or Widowed With No Children

Will Form 5. All-Purpose Will

Beneficiary Worksheet

Self-Proving Affidavits

Self-Proving Affidavit: Form 1

Self-Proving Affidavit: Form 2

Self-Proving Affidavit: Texas

Self-Proving Affidavit: Pennsylvania

Will Codicil Form

Will Form 1. Married With Child(ren), Property to Spouse

Will of ______________________________

I, ____,

a resident of ______________________________, State of ______________________________,

declare that this is my will.

1. Revocation. I revoke all wills that I have previously made.

2. Marital Status. I am married to ______________________________.

3. Children. I have the following child(ren):

Name	Date of Birth

If I do not leave property to one or more of the children or grandchildren whom I have identified above, my failure to do so is intentional.

4. Specific Gifts. I make the following specific gifts of property:

I leave ____

____

____

to ____

or, if such beneficiary(ies) do(es) not survive me, to ______________________________

____.

I leave ____

____

____

to ____

or, if such beneficiary(ies) do(es) not survive me, to ______________________________

____.

I leave ____

____

____

to ____

or, if such beneficiary(ies) do(es) not survive me, to ______________________________________

____.

Any specific gift made in this will to two or more beneficiaries shall be shared equally among them, unless unequal shares are specifically indicated. All shared gifts must be sold, and the net proceeds distributed as the will directs, unless all beneficiaries for that gift agree in writing, after the will writer's death, that a particular gift need not be sold.

If I name two or more primary beneficiaries to receive a specific gift of property and any of them do not survive me, all surviving primary beneficiaries shall equally divide the deceased primary beneficiary's share, unless I have specifically provided otherwise. If I name two or more alternate beneficiaries to receive a specific gift of property and any of them do not survive me, all surviving alternate beneficiaries shall equally divide the deceased alternate beneficiary's share.

5. Residuary Estate. I leave my residuary estate, that is, the rest of my property not otherwise specifically and validly disposed of by this will or in any other manner, including lapsed or failed gifts, to my spouse,

____, or, if my spouse does not survive me, to my child(ren)

____

____.

If I name two or more children as alternate residuary beneficiaries to receive property and any of them do not survive me, all surviving alternate residuary beneficiaries shall equally divide the deceased alternate residuary beneficiary's share.

As used in any section of this will, the word "survive" means to outlive the will writer by at least 45 days.

6. Executor. I name ____

as executor, to serve without bond. If that executor does not qualify, or ceases to serve, I name

____

as executor, also to serve without bond.

I direct that my executor take all actions legally permissible to probate this will, including filing a petition in the appropriate court for the independent administration of my estate.

I grant to my executor the following powers, to be exercised as the executor deems to be in the best interests of my estate:

(1) To retain property, without liability for loss or depreciation resulting from such retention.

(2) To sell, lease or exchange property and to receive or administer the proceeds as a part of my estate.

(3) To vote stock; convert bonds, notes, stocks or other securities belonging to my estate into other securities; and exercise all other rights and privileges of a person owning similar property.

(4) To deal with and settle claims in favor of or against my estate.

(5) To continue, maintain, operate or participate in any business that is a part of my estate, and to incorporate, dissolve or otherwise change the form of organization of the business.

(6) To pay all debts and taxes that may be assessed against my estate, as provided under state law.

(7) To do all other acts which in the executor's judgment may be necessary or appropriate for the proper and advantageous management, investment and distribution of my estate.

These powers, authority and discretion are in addition to the powers, authority and discretion vested in an executor by operation of law, and may be exercised as often as deemed necessary, without approval by any court in any jurisdiction.

7. Personal Guardian. If at my death any of my children are minors and a personal guardian is needed, I name ______________________________ as the personal guardian, to serve without bond. If this person is unable or unwilling to serve as personal guardian, I name ______________________________ as personal guardian, also to serve without bond.

8. Property Guardian. If any of my children are minors and a property guardian is needed, I name ______________________________ as the property guardian, to serve without bond. If this person is unable or unwilling to serve as property guardian, I name ______________________________ as property guardian, also to serve without bond.

9. Children's Trust. All property I leave in this will to any of the beneficiaries listed in Section A, below, shall be held for each of them in a separate trust, administered according to the following terms:

A. Trust Beneficiaries and Age Limits

Each trust shall end when the following beneficiaries become 35 years of age, except as otherwise specified in this section.

Trust Beneficiary	*Trust Shall End at Age*
______________________	____________
______________________	____________
______________________	____________
______________________	____________
______________________	____________

B. Trustees

I name ____

as trustee, to serve without bond. If this person is unable or unwilling to serve as trustee, I name

______________________________________ as successor trustee, also to serve without bond.

C. Beneficiary Provisions

(1) The trustee may distribute for the benefit of each beneficiary as much of the net income or principal of the trust as the trustee deems necessary for the beneficiary's health, support, maintenance and education. In deciding whether to make a distribution for or to a beneficiary, the trustee may take into account the beneficiary's other income, resources and sources of support.

(2) Any trust income that is not distributed to a beneficiary by the trustee shall be accumulated and added to the principal of the trust administered for that beneficiary.

D. Termination of Trust

The trust shall terminate when any of the following occurs:

(1) The beneficiary becomes the age specified in Paragraph A of this trust;

(2) The beneficiary dies before becoming the age specified in Paragraph A of this trust; or

(3) The trust property is used up through distributions allowed under these provisions.

If the trust terminates because the beneficiary reaches the specified age, the remaining principal and accumulated net income of the trust shall pass to the beneficiary. If the trust terminates because the beneficiary dies, the remaining principal and accumulated net income of the trust shall pass to the trust beneficiary's heirs.

E. Powers of Trustee

In addition to other powers granted to the trustee in this will, the trustee shall have:

(1) All the powers generally conferred on trustees by the laws of the state having jurisdiction over this trust;

(2) With respect to property in the trust, the powers conferred by this will on the executor; and

(3) The authority to hire and pay from the trust assets the reasonable fees of investment advisors, accountants, tax advisors, agents, attorneys and other assistants to administer the trust and manage any trust asset and for any litigation affecting the trust.

F. Trust Administration Provisions

(1) This trust shall be administered independent of court supervision to the maximum extent possible under the laws of the state having jurisdiction over this trust.

(2) The interests of trust beneficiaries shall not be transferable by voluntary or involuntary assignment or by operation of law and shall be free from the claims of creditors and from attachment, execution, bankruptcy or other legal process to the fullest extent permissible by law.

(3) Any trustee serving shall be entitled to reasonable compensation out of the trust assets for ordinary and extraordinary services, and for all services in connection with the complete or partial termination of any trust created by this will.

(4) The invalidity of any provision of this trust instrument shall not affect the validity of the remaining provisions.

I subscribe my name to this will this ____________________ day of ____________________, 20_____, at ____, State of ____________________, and declare it is my will, that I sign it willingly, that I execute it as my free and voluntary act for the purposes expressed and that I am of the age of majority or otherwise legally empowered to make a will and under no constraint or undue influence.

____
Signature

Witnesses

On this ______________________ day of ______________________________, 20____, the testator, ____, declared to us, the undersigned, that this instrument was his or her will and requested us to act as witnesses to it. The testator signed this will in our presence, all of us being present at the same time. We now, at the testator's request, in the testator's presence and in the presence of each other, subscribe our names as witnesses and each declare that we are of sound mind and of proper age to witness a will. We further declare that we understand this to be the testator's will, and that to the best of our knowledge the testator is of the age of majority, or is otherwise legally empowered to make a will, and appears to be of sound mind and under no constraint or undue influence.

We declare under penalty of perjury that the foregoing is true and correct, this ________________________ day of ________________________________, 20____, at ____,

State of ____.

______________________________ ______________________________

Witness's Signature Typed or Printed Name

residing at ______________________________, ______________________________,

Street Address City

______________________________, ______________________________.

County State

______________________________ ______________________________

Witness's Signature Typed or Printed Name

residing at ______________________________, ______________________________,

Street Address City

______________________________, ______________________________.

County State

Will Form 2. Married With No Children

Will of ______________________________

I, ______________________________,

a resident of ______________________________, State of ______________________________,

declare that this is my will.

1. Revocation. I revoke all wills that I have previously made.

2. Marital Status. I am married to ______________________________.

3. Specific Gifts. I make the following specific gifts of property:

I leave ______________________________

____

____

to ______________________________

or, if such beneficiary(ies) do(es) not survive me, to ______________________________

______________________________.

I leave ______________________________

____

____

to ______________________________

or, if such beneficiary(ies) do(es) not survive me, to ______________________________

______________________________.

I leave ______________________________

____

____

to ______________________________

or, if such beneficiary(ies) do(es) not survive me, to ______________________________

______________________________.

I leave ____

____

____

to ____

or, if such beneficiary(ies) do(es) not survive me, to ____

____.

Any specific gift made in this will to two or more beneficiaries shall be shared equally among them, unless unequal shares are specifically indicated. All shared gifts must be sold, and the net proceeds distributed as the will directs, unless all beneficiaries for a particular gift agree in writing, after the will writer's death, that the gift need not be sold.

If I name two or more primary beneficiaries to receive a specific gift of property and any of them do not survive me, all surviving primary beneficiaries shall equally divide the deceased primary beneficiary's share, unless I have specifically provided otherwise. If I name two or more alternate beneficiaries to receive a specific gift of property and any of them do not survive me, all surviving alternate beneficiaries shall equally divide the deceased alternate beneficiary's share.

4. Residuary Estate. I leave my residuary estate, that is, the rest of my property not otherwise specifically and validly disposed of by this will or in any other manner, including lapsed or failed gifts, to ______________________________ or, if such residuary beneficiary(ies) do(es) not survive me, to ____

____.

Any residuary gift made in this will to two or more beneficiaries shall be shared equally among them, unless unequal shares are specifically indicated. All shared residuary gifts must be sold, and the net proceeds distributed as the will directs, unless all beneficiaries for a particular gift agree in writing, after the will writer's death, that the gift need not be sold.

If I name two or more alternate residuary beneficiaries to receive property and any of them do not survive me, all surviving alternate residuary beneficiaries shall equally divide the deceased alternate residuary beneficiary's share.

As used in any section of this will, the word "survive" means to outlive the will writer by at least 45 days.

5. Executor. I name ______________________________ as executor, to serve without bond. If that executor does not qualify, or ceases to serve, I name ______________________________ as executor, also to serve without bond.

I direct that my executor take all actions legally permissible to probate this will, including filing a petition in the appropriate court for the independent administration of my estate.

I grant to my executor the following powers, to be exercised as the executor deems to be in the best interests of my estate:

(1) To retain property, without liability for loss or depreciation resulting from such retention.

(2) To sell, lease or exchange property and to receive or administer the proceeds as a part of my estate.

(3) To vote stock; convert bonds, notes, stocks or other securities belonging to my estate into other securities; and exercise all other rights and privileges of a person owning similar property.

(4) To deal with and settle claims in favor of or against my estate.

(5) To continue, maintain, operate or participate in any business that is a part of my estate, and to incorporate, dissolve or otherwise change the form of organization of the business.

(6) To pay all debts and taxes that may be assessed against my estate, as provided under state law.

(7) To do all other acts which in the executor's judgment may be necessary or appropriate for the proper and advantageous management, investment and distribution of my estate.

These powers, authority and discretion are in addition to the powers, authority and discretion vested in an executor by operation of law, and may be exercised as often as deemed necessary, without approval by any court in any jurisdiction.

I subscribe my name to this will this ____________________ day of ____________________, 20____,

at ____, State of ____________________,

and declare it is my will, that I sign it willingly, that I execute it as my free and voluntary act for the purposes expressed and that I am of the age of majority or otherwise legally empowered to make a will and under no constraint or undue influence.

____

Signature

Witnesses

On this ______________ day of ______________________, 20____, the testator, ____, declared to us, the undersigned, that this instrument was his or her will and requested us to act as witnesses to it. The testator signed this will in our presence, all of us being present at the same time. We now, at the testator's request, in the testator's presence and in the presence of each other, subscribe our names as witnesses and each declare that we are of sound mind and of proper age to witness a will. We further declare that we understand this to be the testator's will, and that to the best of our knowledge the testator is of the age of majority, or is otherwise legally empowered to make a will, and appears to be of sound mind and under no constraint or undue influence.

We declare under penalty of perjury that the foregoing is true and correct, this ______________ day of ______________________, 20____, at ______________________________, State of ______________________.

______________________________ ______________________________
Witness's Signature Typed or Printed Name

residing at ______________________________, ______________________________,
Street Address City

______________________________, ______________________________.
County State

______________________________ ______________________________
Witness's Signature Typed or Printed Name

residing at ______________________________, ______________________________,
Street Address City

______________________________, ______________________________.
County State

Will Form 3. Single, Divorced, or Widowed With Child(ren)

Will of ______________________________

I, ____,

a resident of ______________________________, State of ______________________________,

declare that this is my will.

1. Revocation. I revoke all wills that I have previously made.

2. Marital Status. I am married to ______________________________.

3. Children. I have the following child(ren):

Name	Date of Birth

If I do not leave property to one or more of the children or grandchildren whom I have identified above, my failure to do so is intentional.

4. Specific Gifts. I make the following specific gifts of property:

I leave ______________________________

____

____

to ______________________________

or, if such beneficiary(ies) do(es) not survive me, to ______________________________

______________________________.

I leave ______________________________

____

____

to ______________________________

or, if such beneficiary(ies) do(es) not survive me, to ______________________________

______________________________.

I leave ____

____

____

to ____

or, if such beneficiary(ies) do(es) not survive me, to ____

____.

I leave ____

____

____

to ____

or, if such beneficiary(ies) do(es) not survive me, to ____

____.

Any specific gift made in this will to two or more beneficiaries shall be shared equally among them, unless unequal shares are specifically indicated. All shared gifts must be sold, and the net proceeds distributed as the will directs, unless all beneficiaries for a particular gift agree in writing, after the will writer's death, that the gift need not be sold.

If I name two or more primary beneficiaries to receive a specific gift of property and any of them do not survive me, all surviving primary beneficiaries shall equally divide the deceased primary beneficiary's share, unless I have specifically provided otherwise. If I name two or more alternate beneficiaries to receive a specific gift of property and any of them do not survive me, all surviving alternate beneficiaries shall equally divide the deceased alternate beneficiary's share.

5. Residuary Estate. I leave my residuary estate, that is, the rest of my property not otherwise specifically and validly disposed of by this will or in any other manner, including lapsed or failed gifts, to ____

____ or, if such residuary beneficiary(ies) do(es) not survive me, to ____

____.

Any residuary gift made in this will to two or more beneficiaries shall be shared equally among them, unless unequal shares are specifically indicated. All shared residuary gifts must be sold, and the net proceeds distributed as the will directs, unless all beneficiaries for a particular gift agree in writing, after the will writer's death, that the gift need not be sold.

If I name two or more alternate residuary beneficiaries to receive property and any of them do not survive me, all surviving alternate residuary beneficiaries shall equally divide the deceased alternate residuary beneficiary's share.

As used in any section of this will, the word "survive" means to outlive the will writer by at least 45 days.

6. Executor. I name ________________________________ as executor, to serve without bond. If that executor does not qualify, or ceases to serve, I name________________________________ as executor, also to serve without bond.

I direct that my executor take all actions legally permissible to probate this will, including filing a petition in the appropriate court for the independent administration of my estate.

I grant to my executor the following powers, to be exercised as the executor deems to be in the best interests of my estate:

(1) To retain property, without liability for loss or depreciation resulting from such retention.

(2) To sell, lease or exchange property and to receive or administer the proceeds as a part of my estate.

(3) To vote stock; convert bonds, notes, stocks or other securities belonging to my estate into other securities; and exercise all other rights and privileges of a person owning similar property.

(4) To deal with and settle claims in favor of or against my estate.

(5) To continue, maintain, operate or participate in any business that is a part of my estate, and to incorporate, dissolve or otherwise change the form of organization of the business.

(6) To pay all debts and taxes that may be assessed against my estate, as provided under state law.

(7) To do all other acts which in the executor's judgment may be necessary or appropriate for the proper and advantageous management, investment and distribution of my estate.

These powers, authority and discretion are in addition to the powers, authority and discretion vested in an executor by operation of law, and may be exercised as often as deemed necessary, without approval by any court in any jurisdiction.

7. Personal Guardian. If at my death any of my children are minors and a personal guardian is needed, I name

____

as the personal guardian, to serve without bond. If this person is unable or unwilling to serve as personal guardian, I name

____

as personal guardian, also to serve without bond.

8. Property Guardian. If any of my children are minors and a property guardian is needed, I name ________________ ________________________ as the property guardian, to serve without bond. If this person is unable or unwilling to serve as property guardian, I name ________________________________ as property guardian, also to serve without bond.

9. Children's Trust. All property I leave in this will to any of the beneficiaries listed in Section A, below, shall be held for each of them in a separate trust, administered according to the following terms:

A. Trust Beneficiaries and Age Limits

Each trust shall end when the following beneficiaries become 35 years of age, except as otherwise specified in this section.

Trust Beneficiary	*Trust Shall End at Age*
______________________	______________
______________________	______________
______________________	______________
______________________	______________
______________________	______________

B. Trustees

I name ____

as trustee, to serve without bond. If this person is unable or unwilling to serve as trustee, I name

______________________________ as successor trustee, also to serve without bond.

C. Beneficiary Provisions

(1) The trustee may distribute for the benefit of each beneficiary as much of the net income or principal of the trust as the trustee deems necessary for the beneficiary's health, support, maintenance and education. In deciding whether to make a distribution for or to a beneficiary, the trustee may take into account the beneficiary's other income, resources and sources of support.

(2) Any trust income that is not distributed to a beneficiary by the trustee shall be accumulated and added to the principal of the trust administered for that beneficiary.

D. Termination of Trust

The trust shall terminate when any of the following occurs:

(1) The beneficiary becomes the age specified in Paragraph A of this trust;

(2) The beneficiary dies before becoming the age specified in Paragraph A of this trust; or

(3) The trust property is used up through distributions allowed under these provisions.

If the trust terminates because the beneficiary reaches the specified age, the remaining principal and accumulated net income of the trust shall pass to the beneficiary. If the trust terminates because the beneficiary dies, the remaining principal and accumulated net income of the trust shall pass to the trust beneficiary's heirs.

E. Powers of Trustee

In addition to other powers granted to the trustee in this will, the trustee shall have:

(1) All the powers generally conferred on trustees by the laws of the state having jurisdiction over this trust;

(2) With respect to property in the trust, the powers conferred by this will on the executor; and

(3) The authority to hire and pay from the trust assets the reasonable fees of investment advisors, accountants, tax advisors, agents, attorneys and other assistants to administer the trust and manage any trust asset and for any litigation affecting the trust.

F. Trust Administration Provisions

(1) This trust shall be administered independent of court supervision to the maximum extent possible under the laws of the state having jurisdiction over this trust.

(2) The interests of trust beneficiaries shall not be transferable by voluntary or involuntary assignment or by operation of law and shall be free from the claims of creditors and from attachment, execution, bankruptcy or other legal process to the fullest extent permissible by law.

(3) Any trustee serving shall be entitled to reasonable compensation out of the trust assets for ordinary and extraordinary services, and for all services in connection with the complete or partial termination of any trust created by this will.

(4) The invalidity of any provision of this trust instrument shall not affect the validity of the remaining provisions.

I subscribe my name to this will this ____________________ day of ________________, 20_____,
at ____, State of
______________________, and declare it is my will, that I sign it willingly, that I execute it as my free and voluntary act for the purposes expressed and that I am of the age of majority or otherwise legally empowered to make a will and under no constraint or undue influence.

____
Signature

Witnesses

On this ______________________________ day of ____, 20______, the testator, ____, declared to us, the undersigned, that this instrument was his or her will and requested us to act as witnesses to it. The testator signed this will in our presence, all of us being present at the same time. We now, at the testator's request, in the testator's presence and in the presence of each other, subscribe our names as witnesses and each declare that we are of sound mind and of proper age to witness a will. We further declare that we understand this to be the testator's will, and that to the best of our knowledge the testator is of the age of majority, or is otherwise legally empowered to make a will, and appears to be of sound mind and under no constraint or undue influence.

We declare under penalty of perjury that the foregoing is true and correct, this ________________________________ day of ____, 20______, at ____, State of ____.

____ ____
Witness's Signature Typed or Printed Name

residing at ____, ____,
Street Address City

____, ____.
County State

____ ____
Witness's Signature Typed or Printed Name

residing at ____, ____,
Street Address City

____, ____.
County State

Will Form 4. Single, Divorced, or Widowed With No Children

Will of ______________________________

I, ____,

a resident of ______________________________, State of ______________________________,

declare that this is my will.

1. Revocation. I revoke all wills that I have previously made.

2. Marital Status. I am not married.

3. Specific Gifts. I make the following specific gifts of property:

I leave ____

____

____

to ____

or, if such beneficiary(ies) do(es) not survive me, to ______________________________

____.

I leave ____

____

____

to ____

or, if such beneficiary(ies) do(es) not survive me, to ______________________________

____.

I leave ____

____

____

to ____

or, if such beneficiary(ies) do(es) not survive me, to ______________________________

____.

I leave ____

____

____

to ____

or, if such beneficiary(ies) do(es) not survive me, to ____

____.

Any specific gift made in this will to two or more beneficiaries shall be shared equally among them, unless unequal shares are specifically indicated. All shared gifts must be sold, and the net proceeds distributed as the will directs, unless all beneficiaries for a particular gift agree in writing, after the will writer's death, that the gift need not be sold.

If I name two or more primary beneficiaries to receive a specific gift of property and any of them do not survive me, all surviving primary beneficiaries shall equally divide the deceased primary beneficiary's share, unless I have specifically provided otherwise. If I name two or more alternate beneficiaries to receive a specific gift of property and any of them do not survive me, all surviving alternate beneficiaries shall equally divide the deceased alternate beneficiary's share.

4. Residuary Estate. I leave my residuary estate, that is, the rest of my property not otherwise specifically and validly disposed of by this will or in any other manner, including lapsed or failed gifts, to ______________________

______________________________________ or, if such residuary beneficiary(ies) do(es) not survive me, to

____.

Any residuary gift made in this will to two or more beneficiaries shall be shared equally among them, unless unequal shares are specifically indicated. All shared residuary gifts must be sold, and the net proceeds distributed as the will directs, unless all beneficiaries for a particular gift agree in writing, after the will writer's death, that the gift need not be sold.

If I name two or more alternate residuary beneficiaries to receive property and any of them do not survive me, all surviving alternate residuary beneficiaries shall equally divide the deceased alternate residuary beneficiary's share.

As used in any section of this will, the word "survive" means to outlive the will writer by at least 45 days.

5. Executor. I name ____

as executor, to serve without bond. If that executor does not qualify, or ceases to serve, I name

____ as executor, also to serve without bond.

I direct that my executor take all actions legally permissible to probate this will, including filing a petition in the appropriate court for the independent administration of my estate.

I grant to my executor the following powers, to be exercised as the executor deems to be in the best interests of my estate:

(1) To retain property, without liability for loss or depreciation resulting from such retention.

(2) To sell, lease or exchange property, and to receive or administer the proceeds as a part of my estate.

(3) To vote stock; convert bonds, notes, stocks or other securities belonging to my estate into other securities; and exercise all other rights and privileges of a person owning similar property.

(4) To deal with and settle claims in favor of or against my estate.

(5) To continue, maintain, operate or participate in any business that is a part of my estate, and to incorporate, dissolve or otherwise change the form of organization of the business.

(6) To pay all debts and taxes that may be assessed against my estate, as provided under state law.

(7) To do all other acts which in the executor's judgment may be necessary or appropriate for the proper and advantageous management, investment and distribution of my estate.

These powers, authority and discretion are in addition to the powers, authority and discretion vested in an executor by operation of law, and may be exercised as often as deemed necessary, without approval by any court in any jurisdiction.

I subscribe my name to this will this ______________________ day of ____________________, 20_____, at ____, State of ______________________________, and declare it is my will, that I sign it willingly, that I execute it as my free and voluntary act for the purposes expressed and that I am of the age of majority or otherwise legally empowered to make a will and under no constraint or undue influence.

____
Signature

Witnesses

On this ______________________ day of ______________________________, 20____, the testator, ____, declared to us, the undersigned, that this instrument was his or her will and requested us to act as witnesses to it. The testator signed this will in our presence, all of us being present at the same time. We now, at the testator's request, in the testator's presence and in the presence of each other, subscribe our names as witnesses and each declare that we are of sound mind and of proper age to witness a will. We further declare that we understand this to be the testator's will, and that to the best of our knowledge the testator is of the age of majority, or is otherwise legally empowered to make a will, and appears to be of sound mind and under no constraint or undue influence.

We declare under penalty of perjury that the foregoing is true and correct, this ______________________ day of ________________________________, 20____, at ____, State of ____.

____ ____
Witness's Signature Typed or Printed Name

residing at ____, ____,
Street Address City

____, ____.
County State

____ ____
Witness's Signature Typed or Printed Name

residing at ____, ____,
Street Address City

____, ____.
County State

Will Form 5. All-Purpose Will

Will of ______________________________

I, ____,
a resident of ______________________________, State of ______________________________,
declare that this is my will.

1. Revocation. I revoke all wills that I have previously made.

2. Marital Status. ____.

3. Children. I have the following child(ren):

Name	Date of Birth
______________________________	______________________________
______________________________	______________________________
______________________________	______________________________

If I do not leave property to one or more of the children or grandchildren whom I have identified above, my failure to do so is intentional.

4. Specific Gifts. I make the following specific gifts of property:

I leave ____
____
____
to ____
or, if such beneficiary(ies) do(es) not survive me, to ______________________________
____.

I leave ____
____
____
to ____
or, if such beneficiary(ies) do(es) not survive me, to ______________________________
____.

I leave ____

____

____

to ____

or, if such beneficiary(ies) do(es) not survive me, to ______________________

____.

I leave ____

____

____

to ____

or, if such beneficiary(ies) do(es) not survive me, to ______________________

____.

Any specific gift made in this will to two or more beneficiaries shall be shared equally among them, unless unequal shares are specifically indicated. All shared gifts must be sold, and the net proceeds distributed as the will directs, unless all beneficiaries for a particular gift agree in writing, after the will writer's death, that the gift need not be sold.

If I name two or more primary beneficiaries to receive a specific gift of property and any of them do not survive me, all surviving primary beneficiaries shall equally divide the deceased primary beneficiary's share, unless I have specifically provided otherwise. If I name two or more alternate beneficiaries to receive a specific gift of property and any of them do not survive me, all surviving alternate beneficiaries shall equally divide the deceased alternate beneficiary's share.

5. Residuary Estate. I leave my residuary estate, that is, the rest of my property not otherwise specifically and validly disposed of by this will or in any other manner, including lapsed or failed gifts, to ______________________

______________________ or, if such residuary beneficiary(ies) do(es) not survive me, to

____.

Any residuary gift made in this will to two or more beneficiaries shall be shared equally among them, unless unequal shares are specifically indicated. All shared residuary gifts must be sold, and the net proceeds distributed as the will directs, unless all beneficiaries for a particular gift agree in writing, after the will writer's death, that the gift need not be sold.

If I name two or more alternate residuary beneficiaries to receive property and any of them do not survive me, all surviving alternate residuary beneficiaries shall equally divide the deceased alternate residuary beneficiary's share.

As used in any section of this will, the word "survive" means to outlive the will writer by at least 45 days.

6. Executor. I name ______________________________

as executor, to serve without bond. If that executor does not qualify, or ceases to serve, I name ______________

______________________________ as executor, also to serve without bond.

I direct that my executor take all actions legally permissible to probate this will, including filing a petition in the appropriate court for the independent administration of my estate.

I grant to my executor the following powers, to be exercised as the executor deems to be in the best interests of my estate:

(1) To retain property, without liability for loss or depreciation resulting from such retention.

(2) To sell, lease or exchange property, and to receive or administer the proceeds as a part of my estate.

(3) To vote stock; convert bonds, notes, stocks or other securities belonging to my estate into other securities, and exercise all other rights and privileges of a person owning similar property.

(4) To deal with and settle claims in favor of or against my estate.

(5) To continue, maintain, operate or participate in any business that is a part of my estate, and to incorporate, dissolve or otherwise change the form of organization of the business.

(6) To pay all debts and taxes that may be assessed against my estate, as provided under state law.

(7) To do all other acts which in the executor's judgment may be necessary or appropriate for the proper and advantageous management, investment and distribution of my estate.

These powers, authority and discretion are in addition to the powers, authority and discretion vested in an executor by operation of law, and may be exercised as often as deemed necessary, without approval by any court in any jurisdiction.

7. Personal Guardian. If at my death any of my children are minors and a personal guardian is needed, I name

______________________________ as the personal guardian, to serve without bond. If this person is unable or unwilling to serve as personal guardian, I name ______________

______________________________ as personal guardian, also to serve without bond.

8. Property Guardian. If any of my children are minors and a property guardian is needed, I name ______________

______________________________ as the property guardian, to serve without bond. If this person is unable or unwilling to serve as property guardian, I name ______________

______________________________ as property guardian, also to serve without bond.

9. Children's Trust. All property I leave in this will to any of the beneficiaries listed in Section A, below, shall be held for each of them in a separate trust, administered according to the following terms:

A. Trust Beneficiaries and Age Limits

Each trust shall end when the following beneficiaries become 35 years of age, except as otherwise specified in this section.

Trust Beneficiary	*Trust Shall End at Age*
______________________________	______________
______________________________	______________
______________________________	______________
______________________________	______________
______________________________	______________

B. Trustees

I name ____

as trustee, to serve without bond. If this person is unable or unwilling to serve as trustee, I name

______________________________________ as successor trustee, also to serve without bond.

C. Beneficiary Provisions

(1) The trustee may distribute for the benefit of each beneficiary as much of the net income or principal of the trust as the trustee deems necessary for the beneficiary's health, support, maintenance and education. In deciding whether to make a distribution for or to a beneficiary, the trustee may take into account the beneficiary's other income, resources and sources of support.

(2) Any trust income that is not distributed to a beneficiary by the trustee shall be accumulated and added to the principal of the trust administered for that beneficiary.

D. Termination of Trust

The trust shall terminate when any of the following occurs:

(1) The beneficiary becomes the age specified in Paragraph A of this trust;

(2) The beneficiary dies before becoming the age specified in Paragraph A of this trust; or

(3) The trust property is used up through distributions allowed under these provisions.

If the trust terminates because the beneficiary reaches the specified age, the remaining principal and accumulated net income of the trust shall pass to the beneficiary. If the trust terminates because the beneficiary dies, the remaining principal and accumulated net income of the trust shall pass to the trust beneficiary's heirs.

E. Powers of Trustee

In addition to other powers granted to the trustee in this will, the trustee shall have:

(1) All the powers generally conferred on trustees by the laws of the state having jurisdiction over this trust;

(2) With respect to property in the trust, the powers conferred by this will on the executor; and

(3) The authority to hire and pay from the trust assets the reasonable fees of investment advisors, accountants, tax advisors, agents, attorneys and other assistants to administer the trust and manage any trust asset and for any litigation affecting the trust.

F. Trust Administration Provisions

(1) This trust shall be administered independent of court supervision to the maximum extent possible under the laws of the state having jurisdiction over this trust.

(2) The interests of trust beneficiaries shall not be transferable by voluntary or involuntary assignment or by operation of law and shall be free from the claims of creditors and from attachment, execution, bankruptcy or other legal process to the fullest extent permissible by law.

(3) Any trustee serving shall be entitled to reasonable compensation out of the trust assets for ordinary and extraordinary services, and for all services in connection with the complete or partial termination of any trust created by this will.

(4) The invalidity of any provision of this trust instrument shall not affect the validity of the remaining provisions.

I subscribe my name to this will this ______________________ day of ____________________, 20______,
at ____, State of
______________________________, and declare it is my will, that I sign it willingly, that I execute it as my free and voluntary act for the purposes expressed and that I am of the age of majority or otherwise legally empowered to make a will and under no constraint or undue influence.

____
Signature

Witnesses

On this ______________________ day of ______________________________, 20____, the testator, ____, declared to us, the undersigned, that this instrument was his or her will and requested us to act as witnesses to it. The testator signed this will in our presence, all of us being present at the same time. We now, at the testator's request, in the testator's presence and in the presence of each other, subscribe our names as witnesses and each declare that we are of sound mind and of proper age to witness a will. We further declare that we understand this to be the testator's will, and that to the best of our knowledge the testator is of the age of majority, or is otherwise legally empowered to make a will, and appears to be of sound mind and under no constraint or undue influence.

We declare under penalty of perjury that the foregoing is true and correct, this ______________________ day of ______________________________, 20____, at ______________________________________, State of ______________________________.

_______________________________________ Witness's Signature

_______________________________________ Typed or Printed Name

residing at _______________________________________, Street Address

_______________________________________, City

_______________________________________, County

_______________________________________. State

_______________________________________ Witness's Signature

_______________________________________ Typed or Printed Name

residing at _______________________________________, Street Address

_______________________________________, City

_______________________________________, County

_______________________________________. State

Beneficiary Worksheet

Property Left	Beneficiaries for Specific Gifts	
	Primary Beneficiary(ies)	Alternate Beneficiary(ies)

Additional Specific Gifts

I leave ____

____

____

to ____

or, if such beneficiary(ies) do(es) not survive me, to ____

____.

I leave ____

____

____

to ____

or, if such beneficiary(ies) do(es) not survive me, to ____

____.

I leave ____

____

____

to ____

or, if such beneficiary(ies) do(es) not survive me, to ____

____.

I leave ____

____

____

to ____

or, if such beneficiary(ies) do(es) not survive me, to ____

____.

I leave ____

____

____

to ____

or, if such beneficiary(ies) do(es) not survive me, to ____

____.

Self-Proving Affidavits

Self-Proving Affidavit: Form 1

For use by residents of: Alabama, Alaska, Arizona, Arkansas, Colorado, Connecticut, Hawaii, Idaho, Illinois, Indiana, Maine, Minnesota, Mississippi, Montana, Nebraska, Nevada, New Mexico, New York, North Dakota, Oregon, South Carolina, South Dakota, Tennessee, Utah, Virginia, Washington, and West Virginia.

Self-Proving Affidavit: Form 2

For use by residents of: Delaware, Florida, Georgia, Iowa, Kansas, Kentucky, Massachusetts, Missouri, New Jersey, North Carolina, Oklahoma, Pennsylvania, Rhode Island, and Wyoming.

Self-Proving Affidavit: Texas

For use by residents of Texas

Self-Proving Affidavit: Pennsylvania

For use by residents of Pennsylvania

Self-Proving Affidavit: Form 1

Affidavit

We, ____,

____,

____ and

____, the

testator and the witnesses, whose names are signed to the attached instrument in those capacities, personally appearing before the undersigned authority and being first duly sworn, declare to the undersigned authority under penalty of perjury that:

(1) the testator declared, signed and executed the instrument as his or her last will;

(2) he or she signed it willingly or directed another to sign for him or her;

(3) he or she executed it as his or her free and voluntary act for the purposes therein expressed; and

(4) each of the witnesses, at the request of the testator, in his or her hearing and presence and in the presence of each other, signed the will as witnesses and that to the best of his or her knowledge the testator was at that time of full legal age, of sound mind and under no constraint or undue influence.

Testator: ____

Witness: ____

Address: ____

Witness: ____

Address: ____

Witness: ____

Address: ____

Subscribed, sworn and acknowledged before me, ________________________________,

a notary public, by ____,

the testator, and by ____,

____

and ____,

the witnesses, this ________day of ________________________________, 20____.

____

Signature of notary public

[NOTARY SEAL] My commission expires: ________________________________

Self-Proving Affidavit: Form 2

Affidavit

STATE OF ______________________________

COUNTY OF ______________________________

I, the undersigned, an officer authorized to administer oaths, certify that ______________________________

______________________________, the testator, and

______________________________,

______________________________ and

______________________________, the witnesses,

whose names are signed to the attached or foregoing instrument and whose signatures appear below, having appeared together before me and having been first duly sworn, each then declared to me that:

1) the attached or foregoing instrument is the last will of the testator;
2) the testator willingly and voluntarily declared, signed and executed the will in the presence of the witnesses;
3) the witnesses signed the will upon request by the testator, in the presence and hearing of the testator and in the presence of each other;
4) to the best knowledge of each witness the testator was, at that time of the signing, of the age of majority (or otherwise legally competent to make a will), of sound mind and under no constraint or undue influence; and
5) each witness was and is competent, and of the proper age to witness a will.

Testator: ______________________________

Witness: ______________________________

Address: ______________________________

Witness: ______________________________

Address: ______________________________

Witness: ______________________________

Address: ______________________________

Subscribed, sworn and acknowledged before me, ______________________________,

a notary public, by ______________________________,

the testator, and by ______________________________,

____

and ______________________________,

the witnesses, this ______ day of ______________________________, 20____.

SIGNED: ______________________________

____

Official capacity of officer

Self-Proving Affidavit: Texas

Affidavit

THE STATE OF TEXAS

COUNTY OF ______________________________

Before me, the undersigned authority, on this day personally appeared ____

____, ____

____, and ____,

known to me to be the testator and the witnesses, respectively, whose names are subscribed to the annexed or foregoing instrument in their respective capacities, and, all of said persons being by me duly sworn, the said ________________________________, testator, declared to me and to the said witnesses in my presence that said instrument is his or her last will and testament, and that he or she had willingly made and executed it as his or her free act and deed; and the said witnesses, each on his or her oath stated to me, in the presence and hearing of the said testator, that the said testator had declared to them that said instrument is his or her last will and testament, and that he or she executed same as such and wanted each of them to sign it as a witness; and upon their oaths each witness stated further that they did sign the same as witnesses in the presence of the said testator and at his or her request; that he or she was at the time eighteen years of age or over (or being under such age, was or had been lawfully married, or was then a member of the armed forces of the United States or an auxiliary thereof or of the Maritime Service) and was of sound mind; and that each of said witnesses was then at least fourteen years of age.

Testator: ____

Witness: ____

Witness: ____

Subscribed and sworn to before me by the said ____, testator, and by the said ____ and ____, witnesses, this _____ day of ______________________________________, 20___.

SIGNED: ____

____

(Official capacity of officer)

Self-Proving Affidavit, Texas

Affidavit

THE STATE OF TEXAS

COUNTY OF ______

[illegible]

Self-Proving Affidavit: Pennsylvania

Acknowledgment

THE STATE OF PENNSYLVANIA

COUNTY OF ______________________________

I, ____, the testator whose name is signed to the attached or foregoing instrument, having been duly qualified according to law, do hereby acknowledge that I signed and executed the instrument as my Last Will; and that I signed it willingly and as my free and voluntary act for the purposes therein expressed.

Sworn to or affirmed and acknowledged before me by ____, the testator, this ______ day of ____________________________________, 20___.

____
(Testator)

____
(Signature of officer)

Affidavit

THE STATE OF PENNSYLVANIA

COUNTY OF ______________________________

We (or I), ____, and ____, the witness(es) whose name(s) are (is) signed to the attached or foregoing instrument, being duly qualified according to law, do depose and say that we were (I was) present and saw the testator sign and execute the instrument as his Last Will; that the testator signed willingly and executed it as his free and voluntary act for the purposes therein expressed; that each subscribing witness in the hearing and sight of the testator signed the will as a witness; and that to the best of our (my) knowledge the testator was at that time 18 or more years of age, of sound mind and under no constraint or undue influence.

Sworn to or affirmed and acknowledged before me by ____ and ____, witness(es), this ______ day of ____, 20___.

____

Witness: Signature, Name, Address

____

Witness: Signature, Name, Address

____

(Signature of officer)

(Seal and official capacity of officer)

Will Codicil Form

First Codicil to the Will of ______________________________

I, ______________________________, a resident of ______________________________,

______________________________, declare this to be the first codicil to my will dated

______________________________, 20____.

FIRST: I revoke the provision of Section ______ of my will that provided:

and substitute the following :

SECOND: I add the following provision to Section ______:

THIRD: In all other respects I confirm and republish my will dated ______________________________, 20____.

Dated ____________________, 20____.

I subscribe my name to this codicil this ______ day of ____________________, 20______, at

______________________________, ______________________________, ______________________________
City County State

and do hereby declare, under penalty of perjury, that I sign and execute this codicil willingly, that I execute it as my free and voluntary act for the purposes therein expressed and that I am of the age of majority or otherwise legally empowered to make a codicil and under no constraint or undue influence.

____
Signature

On this ______ day of __________________________, 20___, ____

declared to us, the undersigned, that this instrument was the codicil to his/her will and requested us to act as witnesses to it. He/She thereupon signed this codicil in our presence, all of us being present at the same time. We now, at his/her request, in his/her presence and in the presence of each other, subscribe our names as witnesses and declare we understand this to be his/her codicil and that to the best of our knowledge he/she is of the age of majority, or is otherwise legally empowered to make a codicil and is under no constraint or undue influence.

We declare under penalty of perjury that the foregoing is true and correct, this ________________________ day of ______________________________, 20_____, at ____, State of ____.

______________________________ Witness's Signature

______________________________ Typed or Printed Name

residing at ______________________________, Street Address ______________________________, City

______________________________, County ______________________________. State

______________________________ Witness's Signature

______________________________ Typed or Printed Name

residing at ______________________________, Street Address ______________________________, City

______________________________, County ______________________________. State

Index

N

O

P

R

S

CATALOG

...more from Nolo

BUSINESS	PRICE	CODE
Business Buyout Agreements (Book w/CD)	$49.99	BSAG
The California Nonprofit Corporation Kit (Binder w/CD)	$69.99	CNP
California Workers' Comp: Take Charge When You're Injured on the Job	$34.99	WORK
The Complete Guide to Buying a Business (Book w/CD)	$24.99	BUYBU
The Complete Guide to Selling a Business (Book w/CD)	$34.99	SELBU
Consultant & Independent Contractor Agreements (Book w/CD)	$29.99	CICA
The Corporate Records Handbook (Book w/CD)	$69.99	CORMI
Create Your Own Employee Handbook (Book w/CD)	$49.99	EMHA
Dealing With Problem Employees	$44.99	PROBM
Deduct It! Lower Your Small Business Taxes	$34.99	DEDU
Effective Fundraising for Nonprofits	$24.99	EFFN
The Employer's Legal Handbook	$39.99	EMPL
The Essential Guide to Family & Medical Leave (Book w/CD)	$39.99	FMLA
The Essential Guide to Federal Employment Laws	$39.99	FEMP
The Essential Guide to Workplace Investigations (Book w/CD)	$39.99	NVST
Every Nonprofit's Guide to Publishing (Book w/CD)	$29.99	EPNO
Form a Partnership (Book w/CD)	$39.99	PART
Form Your Own Limited Liability Company (Book w/CD)	$44.99	LIAB
Home Business Tax Deductions: Keep What You Earn	$34.99	DEHB
How to Form a Nonprofit Corporation (Book w/CD)—National Edition	$49.99	NNP
How to Form a Nonprofit Corporation in California (Book w/CD)	$49.99	NON
How to Form Your Own California Corporation (Binder w/CD)	$59.99	CACI
How to Form Your Own California Corporation (Book w/CD)	$39.99	CCOR
How to Run a Thriving Business	$19.99	THRV
How to Write a Business Plan (Book w/CD)	$34.99	SBS
Incorporate Your Business (Book w/CD)	$49.99	NIBS
Investors in Your Backyard (Book w/CD)	$24.99	FINBUS
The Job Description Handbook (Book w/CD)	$29.99	JOB
Legal Guide for Starting & Running a Small Business	$34.99	RUNS
Legal Forms for Starting & Running a Small Business (Book w/CD)	$29.99	RUNSF
LLC or Corporation?	$24.99	CHENT
The Manager's Legal Handbook	$39.99	ELBA
Marketing Without Advertising	$20.00	MWAD

Prices subject to change.

BUSINESS (CONTINUED)

	PRICE	CODE
Music Law: How to Run Your Band's Business (Book w/CD)	$39.99	ML
Negotiate the Best Lease for Your Business	$24.99	LESP
Nolo's Quick LLC	$29.99	LLCQ
The Performance Appraisal Handbook (Book w/CD)	$29.99	PERF
The Progressive Discipline Handbook (Book w/CD)	$34.99	SDHB
Small Business in Paradise: Working for Yourself in a Place You Love	$19.99	SPAR
The Small Business Start-up Kit (Book w/CD)—National Edition	$29.99	SMBU
The Small Business Start-up Kit for California (Book w/CD)	$29.99	OPEN
Starting & Building a Nonprofit: A Practical Guide (Book w/CD)	$29.99	SNON
Starting & Running a Successful Newsletter or Magazine	$29.99	MAG
Tax Deductions for Professionals	$34.99	DEPO
Tax Savvy for Small Business	$36.99	SAVVY
The Work from Home Handbook	$19.99	US-HOM
Wow! I'm in Business	$19.99	WHOO
Working for Yourself: Law & Taxes for Independent Contractors, Freelancers & Consultants	$39.99	WAGE
Working With Independent Contractors (Book w/CD)	$29.99	HICI
Your Limited Liability Company: An Operating Manual (Book w/CD)	$49.99	LOP
Your Rights in the Workplace	$29.99	YRW

CONSUMER

How to Win Your Personal Injury Claim	$29.99	PICL
Nolo's Encyclopedia of Everyday Law	$29.99	EVL
Nolo's Guide to California Law	$24.99	CLAW
Your Little Legal Companion (Hardcover)	$9.95	ANNI

ESTATE PLANNING & PROBATE

8 Ways to Avoid Probate	$19.99	PRAV
The Busy Family's Guide to Estate Planning (Book w/CD)	$24.99	FAM
Estate Planning Basics	$21.99	ESPN
The Executor's Guide: Settling a Loved One's Estate or Trust	$39.99	EXEC
Get It Together: Organize Your Records So Your Family Won't Have To (Book w/CD)	$21.99	GET
How to Probate an Estate in California	$49.99	PAE
Make Your Own Living Trust (Book w/CD)	$39.99	LITR
Nolo's Simple Will Book (Book w/CD)	$36.99	SWIL
Plan Your Estate	$44.99	NEST
Quick & Legal Will Book (Book w/CD)	$19.99	QUIC
Special Needs Trusts: Protect Your Child's Financial Future (Book w/CD)	$34.99	SPNT

FAMILY MATTERS

	PRICE	CODE
Always Dad: Being a Great Father During & After a Divorce	$16.99	DIFA
Building a Parenting Agreement That Works	$24.99	CUST
The Complete IEP Guide	$34.99	IEP
Divorce & Money: How to Make the Best Financial Decisions During Divorce	$34.99	DIMO
Divorce Without Court: A Guide to Mediation & Collaborative Divorce	$29.99	DWCT
Do Your Own California Adoption: Nolo's Guide for Stepparents & Domestic Partners (Book w/CD)	$34.99	ADOP
Every Dog's Legal Guide: A Must-Have for Your Owner	$19.99	DOG
The Guardianship Book for California	$34.99	GB
A Judge's Guide to Divorce (Book w/CD)	$24.99	JDIV
A Legal Guide for Lesbian and Gay Couples (Book w/CD)	$34.99	LG
Living Together: A Legal Guide for Unmarried Couples (Book w/CD)	$34.99	LTK
Nolo's Essential Guide to Divorce	$24.99	NODV
Nolo's IEP Guide: Learning Disabilities	$29.99	IELD
Parent Savvy	$19.99	PRNT
Prenuptial Agreements: How to Write a Fair & Lasting Contract (Book w/CD)	$34.99	PNUP

GOING TO COURT

Becoming a Mediator	$29.99	BECM
Beat Your Ticket: Go To Court & Win!—National Edition	$21.99	BEYT
The Criminal Law Handbook: Know Your Rights, Survive the System	$39.99	KYR
Everybody's Guide to Small Claims Court—National Edition	$29.99	NSCC
Everybody's Guide to Small Claims Court in California	$29.99	CSCC
Fight Your Ticket & Win in California	$29.99	FYT
How to Change Your Name in California	$34.99	NAME
Legal Research: How to Find & Understand the Law	$39.99	LRES
Nolo's Deposition Handbook	$34.99	DEP
Represent Yourself in Court: How to Prepare & Try a Winning Case	$39.99	RYC
Win Your Lawsuit: A Judge's Guide to Representing Yourself in California Superior Court	$39.99	SLWY

HOMEOWNERS, LANDLORDS & TENANTS

Buying a Second Home (Book w/CD)	$24.99	SCND
The California Landlord's Law Book: Evictions (Book w/CD)	$44.99	LBEV
The California Landlord's Law Book: Rights & Responsibilities (Book w/CD)	$44.99	LBRT
California Tenants' Rights	$29.99	CTEN
Deeds for California Real Estate	$27.99	DEED
Every Landlord's Guide to Finding Great Tenants (Book w/CD)	$19.99	FIND

HOMEOWNERS, LANDLORDS & TENANTS (CONTINUED)	PRICE	CODE
Every Landlord's Legal Guide (Book w/CD)—National Edition	$44.99	ELLI
Every Landlord's Property Protection Guide (Book w/CD)	$29.99	RISK
Every Landlord's Tax Deduction Guide	$34.99	DELL
Every Tenant's Legal Guide—National Edition	$29.99	EVTEN
For Sale by Owner in California (Book w/CD)	$29.99	FSBO
How to Buy a House in California	$34.99	BHCA
Leases & Rental Agreements (Book w/CD)	$29.99	LEAR
Neighbor Law: Fences, Trees, Boundaries & Noise	$29.99	NEI
Nolo's Essential Guide to Buying Your First Home (Book w/CD)	$24.99	HTBH
Renters' Rights: The Basics	$24.99	RENT

IMMIGRATION

Becoming A U.S. Citizen: A Guide to the Law, Exam & Interview	$24.99	USCIT
Fiancé & Marriage Visas	$34.99	IMAR
How to Get a Green Card	$29.99	GRN
U.S. Immigration Made Easy	$39.99	IMEZ

MONEY MATTERS

101 Law Forms for Personal Use (Book w/CD)	$29.99	SPOT
The Busy Family's Guide to Money	$19.99	US-MONY
Chapter 13 Bankruptcy: Repay Your Debts	$39.99	CHB
Credit Repair (Book w/CD)	$24.99	CREP
How to File for Chapter 7 Bankruptcy	$29.99	HFB
IRAs, 401(k)s & Other Retirement Plans: Taking Your Money Out	$34.99	RET
Lower Taxes in 7 Easy Steps	$16.99	LTAX
The New Bankruptcy: Will It Work for You?	$21.99	FIBA
Nolo's Guide to Social Security Disability (Book w/CD)	$29.99	QSS
Solve Your Money Troubles	$19.99	MT
Stand Up to the IRS	$29.99	SIRS
Surviving an IRS Tax Audit	$24.95	SAUD

PATENTS AND COPYRIGHTS

All I Need is Money: How to Finance Your Invention	$19.99	FINA
The Copyright Handbook: What Every Writer Needs to Know (Book w/CD)	$39.99	COHA
Getting Permission: How to License and Clear Copyrighted Materials (Book w/CD)	$34.99	RIPER
How to Make Patent Drawings	$29.99	DRAW
The Inventor's Notebook	$24.99	INOT

PATENTS AND COPYRIGHTS (CONTINUED)

	PRICE	CODE
Legal Guide to Web & Software Development (Book w/CD)	$44.99	SFT
Nolo's Patents for Beginners	$24.99	QPAT
Patent, Copyright & Trademark: An Intellectual Property Desk Reference	$39.99	PCTM
Patent It Yourself	$49.99	PAT
Patent Pending in 24 Hours	$34.99	PEND
Patent Savvy for Managers: Spot & Protect Valuable Innovations in Your Company	$29.99	PATM
Patenting Art & Entertainment: New Strategies for Protecting Creative Ideas	$39.99	PATAE
Profit from Your Idea (Book w/CD)	$34.99	LICE
The Public Domain	$34.99	PUBL
Trademark: Legal Care for Your Business and Product Name	$39.99	TRD
What Every Inventor Needs to Know About Business & Taxes (Book w/CD)	$21.99	ILAX

RETIREMENT & SENIORS

Get a Life: You Don't Need a Million to Retire Well	$24.99	LIFE
Long-Term Care: How to Plan & Pay for It	$19.99	ELD
Retire Happy	$19.99	US-RICH
Social Security, Medicare & Goverment Pensions	$29.99	SOA
Work Less, Live More: The Way to Semi-Retirement	$17.99	RECL
The Work Less, Live More Workbook (Book w/CD)	$19.99	RECW

SOFTWARE

Call or check our website at www.nolo.com for special discounts on Software!

Leasewriter Plus 2.0—Windows	$49.99	LWD2
LLC Maker—Windows	$69.99	LLP1
Patent Pending Now!—Windows	$89.99	PP1
PatentEase 6.0—Windows	$259.00	PEAS
Personal RecordKeeper 5.0—Windows	$39.99	RKD5
Quicken Legal Business Pro 2008—Windows	$79.99	SBQB8
Quicken WillMaker Plus 2008—Windows	$49.99	WQP8

Special Upgrade Offer

Save 35% on the latest edition of your Nolo book

Because laws and legal procedures change often, we update our books regularly. To help keep you up-to-date, we are extending this special upgrade offer. Cut out and mail the title portion of the cover of your old Nolo book and we'll give you 35% off the retail price of the New Edition of that book when you purchase directly from Nolo. This offer is to individuals only.

Order Form

Name	
Address	
City	
State, Zip	
Daytime Phone	
E-mail	

Our "No-Hassle" Guarantee

Return anything you buy directly from Nolo for any reason and we'll cheerfully refund your purchase price. No ifs, ands or buts.

☐ Check here if you do not wish to receive mailings from other companies

Item Code	Quantity	Item	Unit Price	Total Price

Method of payment

☐ Check ☐ VISA
☐ American Express
☐ MasterCard
☐ Discover Card

Subtotal	
Add your local sales tax (California only)	
Shipping: RUSH $12, Basic $6 (See below)	
"I bought 2, ship it to me FREE!"(Ground shipping only)	
TOTAL	

Account Number

Expiration Date

Signature

Shipping and Handling

Rush Delivery—Only $12

We'll ship any order to any street address in the U.S. by UPS 2nd Day Air* for only $12!

* Order by 9:30 AM Pacific Time and get your order in 2 business days. Orders placed after 9:30 AM Pacific Time will arrive in 3 business days. P.O. boxes and S.F. Bay Area use basic shipping. Alaska and Hawaii use 2nd Day Air or Priority Mail.

Basic Shipping—$6

Use for P.O. Boxes, Northern California and Ground Service.

Allow 1-2 weeks for delivery.

U.S. addresses only.

For faster service, use your credit card and our toll-free numbers

Call our customer service group Monday thru Friday 7am to 7pm PST

Phone
1-800-728-3555

Fax
1-800-645-0895

Mail
Nolo
950 Parker St.
Berkeley, CA 94710

NOLO

Order 24 hours a day @ www.nolo.com

Get the Latest in the Law

Nolo's Legal Updater
We'll send you an email whenever a new edition of your book is published! Sign up at **www.nolo.com/legalupdater**.

Updates at Nolo.com
Check **www.nolo.com/update** to find recent changes in the law that affect the current edition of your book.

Nolo Customer Service
To make sure that this edition of the book is the most recent one, call us at **800-728-3555** and ask one of our friendly customer service representatives (7:00 am to 6:00 pm PST, weekdays only). Or find out at **www.nolo.com**.

Complete the Registration & Comment Card ...
... and we'll do the work for you! Just indicate your preferences below:

Registration & Comment Card

NAME DATE

ADDRESS

CITY STATE ZIP

PHONE EMAIL

COMMENTS

WAS THIS BOOK EASY TO USE? (VERY EASY) 5 4 3 2 1 (VERY DIFFICULT)

☐ Yes, you can quote me in future Nolo promotional materials. *Please include phone number above.*

☐ Yes, send me **Nolo's Legal Updater** via email when a new edition of this book is available.

Yes, I want to sign up for the following email newsletters:

- ☐ **NoloBriefs** (monthly)
- ☐ **Nolo's Special Offer** (monthly)
- ☐ **Nolo's BizBriefs** (monthly)
- ☐ **Every Landlord's Quarterly** (four times a year)

QUIC5

☐ Yes, you can give my contact info to carefully selected partners whose products may be of interest to me.

Send to: **Nolo** 950 Parker Street, Berkeley, CA 94710-9867, Fax: (800) 645-0895, or include all of the above information in an email to regcard@nolo.com with the subject line "QUIC5."